I PLEDGE ALLEGIANCE…

An anthology of stories and feelings of the members
of the Wednesday Warrior Writers in honor of the
Heroes and Patriots of the United States of America

Wednesday Warrior Writers

I Pledge Allegiance…
By
Members of
Wednesday Warrior Writers © 2012

All rights reserved with the following exception: Any part of this book may be reproduced or used for educational or civic functions at the discretion of the purchaser provided credit is given to the original author along with the title of this book and the Publisher of this book without obtaining the advance consent of either the Author or the Publisher.

ISBN: 978-1-936759-13-2

Second Edition

Proudly published in the United States of America in cooperation with Houdini Publishing

HOUDINI™
PUBLISHING
houdinipublishing.com

TABLE OF CONTENTS

A Father and Son Last Trip	3
A Hero is Gone	7
Are Patriots Heroes and Vice-Versa	11
Waller J. Parker, A Chosin One	17
Dogs of War	25
Patriots of WWII	31
One of the Proud, the Few	37
The Flag on the Mountain	41
Shootout	45
A Nation of Belief	53
Amongst the Shadow and the Stones	57
An Early Hero	63
Not All Heroes Get Medals	67
On Patriotism	73
Scars of the Heart	77
Tears of the heart	85
Sharks and Heroes Made of Steel	95
Those Daring Young Men	99

Viva La Troop	105
Weekend Warriors	109
French Davis	117
Angels Also Get Bronze Stars	123
The Atrocity of War	127
Audie Murphy	129
Police Officer Eddie Byrne Memorial	137
Every Family Has a Hero or a Patriot	143
Farewell to a Fireman	151
Family Traits	155
Joseph Marion "Ian" Moore	159
The Medal of Honor	165
Patriots and Heroes	169
President's Day	173
Richard Allen Kerr	177
A Foot Ahead	179
Buried Alive	183
Eric Dixon's Fourth of July	187
I Am an American and Proud of It	191
I Met a Hero Today	195

Thomas Edgar "Jock" Clifford	199
Heroes, Patriots and Victims	203
Lost and Found	209
Memories in Green	215
Our Monument At Last	219
Takeover	225
The Youngest Hero	237
What Was Your Name Doc?	241
Where Is Our Patriotism	245
Bob Hope – Patriot	249
Paid in Full	253
What Was It Like When	257
Power of the American Press (IMO)	261
The Day the Old Detective Cried	265
Where There's Hope	269
The Shrine in Las Vegas	275
What is a Hero?	281
Why We Attend	283

DEDICATION

This book is dedicated to all veterans of all military services, past, present and future. It is they who have and will have allowed us to live in a free society through their sacrifices. As individuals we must thank them, and as a nation we must take care of them as certainly as they took care of us.

As members of the Wednesday Warrior Writers of Las Vegas Nevada, we have authored this book. It is our opinions of who some of the known and lesser known heroes and patriots are. We promise that all proceeds of this book will be donated to a 501 (c) (3) registered organization whose stated mission is to help veterans of military service along with their families.

Any such organization may submit their application to receive proceeds from the sale of this book by applying by letter to the publisher of this book, Houdini Publications, 6455 Dean Martin Drive suite I, Las Vegas Nevada 89118. The publisher will forward all applications to a member of the Wednesday Warrior Writers for consideration.

INTRODUCTION

The Wednesday Warrior Writers is a group of friends with a common desire to write. We toiled over the name for our small group and settled on Warriors because we are former military or former first responders. We meet on Wednesdays and Wednesday First Responders just didn't click. It sounded as though we would only respond to emergencies on Wednesdays. Thus we settled on Wednesday Warrior Writers.

We have another thing in common also. We all share a deep and abiding love for our country, The United States of America.

One of our members, Merle Savage was a friend and author of Silence in the Sound. She was a mother and grandmother and interesting lady. She was a foreman at the Exxon Valdez oil spill in Alaska. Although small in stature she was a giant when she supervised big men doing the cleanup forcing them to do their jobs properly. Merle's son is a career military man and a Master Sergeant still on active duty. Merles' Grandson also served. He completed a tour in Iraq and returned to the States only to be killed in a heartbreaking motorcycle accident in South Carolina. Merle's son travelled in uniform to South Carolina to return his sons cremains for burial. He wrote his mother about the trip and Merle shared the letter with us. This letter was so moving to us that we decided that he and other sung and unsung heroes should be memorialized. Thus, being writers, this is the way we did it.

Merle is no longer with us although she did fulfill an item on her bucket list. She wanted to see her birthday on 11-11-11 and she did surrounded by her friends and family.

"I Pledge Allegiance..." begins with Merles' letter from her son. The rest of this book is other stories, thoughts, and feelings of the members of the Wednesday Warrior Writers.

We hope you enjoy this work of respect and love for country; and stand with us in "Pledging Allegiance" to our flag and country; and to all that have served her. For us, we were lucky and fortunate to have been born in America, the greatest country in the world and the country we Pledge Allegiance to.

For more information about the photo used for the cover of this book, read Eric Dixon's Fourth of July on page 189.

A FATHER AND SONS LAST TRIP

Offered to Merle Savage by her son, the father of

Alex Michael Savage

Please let me spend a few moments telling you about our trip home. After packing Alex's gear and a little of his personal items they were loaded into my rental car. When I got to the airport, Alex, in true style, didn't want to leave. I loaded his bags onto the cart, clutched his remains in my arms and attempted to push his bags through the airport. Well the bags managed to turn left and then turn right and proceed to fall off the cart.

"Alex, come on buddy, not right now, we need to go home."

An old marine came over and gave me a larger cart and offered to assist.

Alex and I arrived at the ticket counter and all was good. Upon entering TSA, the officer instructed me to place my belongings onto the machine. As I was escorting Alex home in uniform, I pulled the gentleman to the side and informed him that I would not place my son onto a belt to be x-rayed and that he needed to bring his supervisor over. She approached and proceeded to tell me the same thing until I told her of my mission. She immediately broke down in tears which caused me to start to lose my "game face." She asked if she could carry Alex over to the screening room and she clutched him as if she was holding her own baby. With tears rolling down her face she placed Alex onto the table and touched the outside of the bag. Then Alex and I moved out.

On the plane I was told "Sir you will need to place your bag in the bin or below your seat" a passenger said to me.

"Hey, I believe I will hold onto my son for this trip."

The man apologized and was somber the rest of the flight and I could hear Alex, "Yeah you dork," (or maybe something more colorful).

Second flight caught us moving out smartly to the gate and again Alex was attempting to get away. The bag provided by the funeral home in Myrtle Beach was splitting down the side.

"Alex, are you serious dude? Come on, will you just come with me and stop playing around?"

The airline assisted with some baggage stickers to hold the bag together and offered me a place to "change Alex's mode of transportation." The USO was called by the airline and they offered the only thing they had, a canvas casino bag.

Again? Really Alex! Poker? Now?

I thanked the former army USO gentleman and told him we would make do with the bag, we are almost home. Alex, always ready to help, carried my lunch and we entered the plane in front of others. We sat down and had a talk silently as others boarded the plane. As the attendants announced departure and started the cross check the door almost closed and the sounds of quick footsteps came bounding down the aisle. It was the USO gentleman carrying a canvas USO bag large enough for Alex. The passenger next to me assisted in the mode of transportation change.

Last flight, Alex and I are on the home stretch. Mind you, I have not held Alex in my arms like a baby for some time and my "game face" was taking its toll on me. As I stood at the counter waiting to board, the gentleman at the counter said he liked my bag, another fellow comrade in arms, I told him that I was escorting my son home. The man's eyes dimmed and he slowly bowed his head and mouthed, "Sorry."

I nodded back...and in true Alex form, a woman next to me said, "Oh how nice you're carrying your baby? Is he in there?"

Her husband in complete horror reached out slowly and touched her shoulder, she looked back at him and I said, "Ma'am I am escorting my son home." She was devastated and we were hugged. "No worries ma'am, but if you keep up the crying, I might breakdown and join you here and no one will board the plane." Alex and I had a great flight and as we landed, my heart had finally reached its limits and quietly I sobbed. As the plane taxied to the gate the flight attendant announced the time, weather and where to claim baggage. Then as we rolled up to the gate they announced that they would like to welcome home a fallen soldier who is being escorted home by his father. They asked all passengers to remain seated until the father and son exited the plane.

"Welcome Home."

A HERO IS GONE

By

Keith Bettinger

The newspaper's obituary column announced that a man named Spann Watson passed away from complications of pneumonia in Winthrop Memorial Hospital in Mineola, N.Y., at the age of ninety-three. Many people didn't know this gentle man, and I regret that I didn't meet him sooner or know him better. You see, Spann Watson was living history. He was a pilot in the United States Army Air Forces during World War II. However, more importantly he was one of the first men picked to be a Tuskegee Airman, a group of African-Americans pilots who proved to the military and to our country, that they were as capable as any white serviceman. He eventually became Lt. Colonel Spann Watson, USAF, Retired; a proud and dignified man worthy of everyone's respect.

In the dark days of World War II and during a time of non-existent civil rights for African-Americans, he fought for the privilege to fight for his country; the same country that denied him the rights that were afforded German prisoners of war who were residing in prisoner of war camps in America. He was even arrested at an Air Force base in Michigan when he and other black pilots had the audacity to enter the "Whites Only" officer's club.

After a distinguished career, he retired from the Air Force, but he wasn't done with the United States government. He went to work for the Federal Aviation Administration for the next thirty years. There he ran a program that looked for and mentored qualified minority applicants. As he was proud of saying, he had a fifty year career in the federal government.

I went to high school with Orin Watson, Colonel Watson's son. Orin was a year ahead of me in school. He went on to follow in his father's career path by attending the United States Air Force Academy and graduating in 1971. During his military career, he flew B-52s for the Air Force. Tragically, he was taken too soon. He died in an automobile collision while attending training to learn to fly Air Force fighter jets.

I had the pleasure of inviting Colonel Watson to be a guest speaker at a meeting of the Shields of Long Island, a fraternal police organization of which I am the secretary. I called his home expecting the usual 'hello'. When he answered the phone, he barked "WATSON HERE!" I thought I was going to jump up out of my chair and stand at attention. I may never have been in the service, but I knew that that voice commanded respect.

I invited him to be a speaker at our meeting at the Swan Club in Glen Head, N. Y. When I arrived, he was there already. He was sitting in his car, wearing a tie and sport jacket waiting for the appointed hour to enter the restaurant. I walked over and introduced myself. As he got out of his car, he removed his driving shoes; an old and worn pair of loafers. He then put on his spit shined military oxfords. Over his shoulder, he carried a sealed clothing bag. Before the meeting, he slipped out of his green sports jacket and put on the famed red blazer of the Tuskegee Airmen, a garment of pride that he carried in the clothing bag. He spoke for almost an hour and received a standing ovation at the end of his presentation. During the quiet times while members ate dinner, Mr. Watson and I shared memories of his son Orin.

At the following annual board meeting of the Shields, we invited him to be an honorary member. We only invite a few special friends to be honorary members. He graciously accepted our invitation and was proud of his membership. Recently, he returned to a Shields meeting at the Stewart Thomas Manor in Plainedge, N. Y. Although he was some years older and physically a little bit slower, he still mesmerized the attendees with his presentation about the exploits of his fellow airmen.

When he was ninety-one years old, he had Lasik surgery and no longer needed glasses. His eyes were strong enough and well enough to return him to the cockpit that he so loved.

The Tuskegee Airmen, living and dead, finally received a prestigious citation for their service, and Colonel

Watson was there to receive his overdue thank you from a grateful nation. He received an invitation to attend the 2009 Presidential Inauguration with other fellow Tuskegee Airmen. What an honor to receive an invitation to attend such an historic event.

Now at age ninety-three, what a war could not do pneumonia has accomplished; it has stolen Lieutenant Colonel Spann Watson from us. The only good thing I can see to come out of this tragedy is that Spann's son, Orin, now has very special wingman at his side to soar upon the heavenly skies.

ARE PATRIOTS HEROES AND VICE VERSA?

By

Jack Miller

I have had the honor to personally meet two heroes who have been awarded the Medal of Honor. That is the highest medal our country bestows on people who have performed heroic acts in combat. The first was in Detroit, Michigan, in 1957 and I am ashamed that I do not remember his name. I'm also ashamed of my conduct at that time. The other was Sergeant Sammy Davis, and I had the honor of meeting him in 2008 on a "Salute to Veterans Cruise" in the Caribbean. The first man was awarded his medal for heroism in Korea, and Sergeant Davis for his acts in the Republic of Vietnam. No doubt these men were heroes and for certain Sergeant Davis is a patriot.

But what is a patriot?

Many have asked that question and some have tried to provide a definitive answer. I don't believe a definitive answer is possible because for each person patriotism is different. For some, it might be the feeling they get when they see a parade with the flags and the marching bands. For others, it might be seeing soldiers, sailors, airmen and marines returning from some war zone and being welcomed by their loved ones. Others still might get a lump in their throat when they hear the Star Spangled Banner or Taps at a military funeral. Patriotism might be shown by a person who displays the flag of the United States on his house during certain days.

Are people patriotic because they have served in the military and belong to a veteran organization which celebrates our country? I believe with all my heart that in all of the above situations, the person can be considered patriotic without being heroic.

Still, for others, patriotism might not even exist until a tragedy occurs. I recall December 7, 1941. Most of the people I knew were angered but most also asked, "Where is Pearl Harbor?" When the Americans learned where Pearl Harbor was and what happened, they flocked to the recruiting stations to volunteer. Mothers, kids and grandparents began eating fish on Tuesdays and Fridays so the GI could have meat. Kids began collecting scrap iron, tin cans and newspapers to be used in the war effort. Everyone who had a son or daughter serving in the armed forces hung a small red and white banner in their window with a blue star representing a serviceman. Some families had as many as five blue stars. Some had their star in gold representing a son killed. Some families like the Sullivans had to turn their five blue stars into five gold ones because they had lost all of their sons. Were they patriots for displaying their banner for heroes or allowing all their sons to go to war? Were they both?

Next we sent our military to Korea to fight "The Forgotten War" because it was called a "Police Action." Our news media barely covered that as news.

Then we sent our military personnel into Vietnam, and most served with dedication and honor. The media on the home front gave attention to the demonstrations of a few protestors who objected to this police action, rather than the patriots. Some demonstrators burned their draft cards, and our flag, and they were shown on the prime time news. It became more newsworthy to record this than to the dedication and honor being displayed by the vast majority of our military. Returning military members, some of whom were true heroes were called names and spit upon because a news camera was close by. Proud members of the military, some of whom had never served anywhere but within the United States were instructed not to wear their uniforms off post lest one of these protestors created a scene in front of a camera. Who were the patriots and who were the heroes? Was it the servicemen or the media reporters?

Then we had another tragedy which brought us together. Almost everyone who is old enough to read this will remember the World Trade Center attack on September 11, 2001. That was a date that most every American felt the call of patriotism. We had been attacked on our own soil. Almost everyone knew where New York City was, and almost everyone I knew was shocked and ready to answer a call to retaliate. We all wanted to be the patriot who revenged this atrocity.

The architect of the attack on Pearl Harbor was General Hideki Tojo who was tried after the war for war crimes and sentenced to death. The sentence was carried out on

23 December 1948 when Tojo was hanged. However, during those "Police Actions" called Korea and Vietnam, it was some members of our own military who were tried and convicted for war crimes. Because a truce was called in Korea and the US withdrew from Vietnam, both situations where the US was not victorious due to political pressure, there was no atonement or trials of any North Korean or North Vietnam Army officers for crimes perpetrated upon our military personnel who were taken prisoner. Their torture and inhumane treatment is a matter of record, yet goes unpunished.

On May 2, 2011 the architect of the destruction of the World Trade Center, Osama Bin Laden, was shot to death by US Navy SEALS. This truly was a patriotic act but we will never know who that particular hero was.

Back to the question of hero versus patriot. I believe that only the winning side can have heroes. Osama Bin Laden and Tojo were both willing to attack the United States for individual reasons and were considered patriotic by their side. Had their side won they would have been considered heroes as well.. Yet in our eyes neither can be considered patriots and certainly not heroes.

Those two Americans I met who were awarded the Medal of Honor were definitely heroes and by the very actions for which the award was made they must be considered patriots as well. The US Navy SEALS can be considered patriots and heroes because they were willing to go as ordered and performed heroically. So to be a hero, a person must do something for another person. To be a patriot, a person must do something for his country and be on the winning side.

An anonymous poet once penned:

> God and the soldier
> All men adore
> In time of trouble,
> And no more;
> For when war is over
> And all things righted,
> God is neglected -
> The soldier slighted.

To be a patriot, a person must be willing to love his country. He must be willing to stand when his flag, the symbol of his beloved country passes by. He must feel the lump in his throat when he says his Pledge of Allegiance; hears the volley of shots saluting a fallen hero or his national anthem. He must respect his service people who are willing to place themselves in harm's way for his country and for him. He must be willing to be proud, proud enough to fight and to win. We can all be patriots. We only have to be willing.

WALLER J. PARKER

"A Chosin One"

By

Charles McKee

I met him the first night I began my attendance with the United States Naval Reserve Electronics Division 12-3, in Richmond, California.

He was tall, husky, and carried himself with purposeful military demeanor. He was after all First Class Hospital Corpsman Medic, Waller J. Parker. He earned our undying respect that caused each and every one of us, the uninitiated Bluejacket, to pattern our behavior in his Navy image.

My exposure to the United States Navy and Marine Corp. was early and often. Many family friends had served in the Second World War aboard fighting ships in the Pacific theater of operations. Several had also served during the Korean War. Many would continue their service to our country as Naval Reservists following our two noteworthy conflicts that affected my early life. Waller Parker was one of those men that left his indelible stamp on me as well as many other young members of the Naval Reserve.

He spoke little of his Navy career, or his personal life. But as I grew into the small Naval Reserve Unit 12-3, in

Shipyard Three, Richmond, California the combat history of Hospital Corpsman Parker was revealed.

He was a local boy, having graduated from Richmond Union High School with the class of 1948.

Waller James Parker graduated with Navy Boot Camp Company 361, San Diego, California, on the seventh of September 1948. And ironically, his Boot Camp Company Commander was Gunners Mate Chief L.A. Parker. All seventy- nine graduates of company 361 would eventually face in some way, the growing conflict on the Korean peninsula.

The fledgling navy bluejacket seemed to possess an interest in the medical and dentistry fields, and would graduate from Navy Corpsman School in February of 1949. As a teenage sailor, I doubt he, or his fellow sailors saw what awaited them just over the horizon in a foreign land.

Understanding that US Navy Corpsmen are the US Marine Corp field medics; now charts the course that will lead Parker and many of his contemporaries and the marines into the Korean conflict.

Many writers and historians refer to Korea as a conflict; but it was still a nasty, cold and bloody war. The United States was still in a five year recovery from World War II that returned many of her sons and daughters to Korea equipped with Second World War equipment and tactics. Waller Parker was recalled to active duty almost to the day from his initial discharge, August 10, 1950.

The new corpsman transited through Treasure Island Naval Base, and a week later found himself at Camp Pendleton Marine Base in San Diego.

With six weeks field medical training completed, it was up to the Marine Corps to outfit the young corpsman with marine uniforms, and basic infantry equipment, also known as 782 gear. The field training began in earnest as the young medics merged into their respective marine training units.

Parker recalls the training as arduous, and absolutely necessary as he would quickly find out once he set foot on Korean soil.

The new corpsman, and fellow corps school graduates; Joe BURKS, Stanley WEAVER, Yolinsky D'LERENZO, Richard SMITH, Denny Le PLANT, Richard HAYES and Gilmer FORDYCE arrived at Camp Otsu, Japan on October 1,1950 for additional training and weapons issuance.

The newly equipped Navy-Marine Corpsmen landed at Wonsan Harbor in the early days of November 1950.

They soon found that travel from Wonsan to Hungnam was going to be difficult as the rail lines were under constant attack by the aggressive North Koreans.

Luck would have it that one of Parker's group was in fact a railroad engineer who would captain the first train to Hungnam with fifty corpsmen aboard. The group met with sporadic fire from the enemy, but this train arrived on time, thanks to the United States Navy.

Hungnam marine units received the new corpsmen into the fifth and seventh Marine regiments. Corpsman Parker joined the 3rd Platoon, Able Company, 1st Battalion, 5th Marine Regiment, at Majon-nee.

Parker's immediate duties were to hold sick call, and provide care for the wounded marines; as the battalions leap frogged Northward toward the Yalu River.

The temperature plummeted below zero degrees and the bitter cold added another enemy to be conquered. Cold weather gear was issued but it often hampered combat troops, and their corpsmen. Parker would later comment that morphine injectors were carried in his mouth to keep them from freezing; and that many of the corpsmen worked without the hindrance of their cold weather gloves. He would also suffer for the remainder of his life from the aftermath of the Korean frostbite.

The fifth Regiment was ordered to join the seventh Regiment at Yudam-ni by way of a torturous truck ride over narrow frozen roads. The exhausted troops dropped to the frozen ground, and slept exactly where they dismounted from the trucks.

At about midnight, Parker was awakened by Tech. Sgt. Milar stating "Come on Doc the gooks have hit the Seventh's position hard; we have to reinforce them."

As the platoons started up to reinforce Easy Company they came under heavy sniper fire about half way up the rocky terrain. The platoons finally reached the ridge, and took up positions across a small sloped ravine which gave quick access to the ridge itself.

The job of protecting the 1st battalion and 5th regimental headquarters located at the foot of the mountainous terrain fell to Parker's unit as well.

As the platoons massed at the ridge they were taken under heavy Chinese small arms and mortars fire. The unit held its position although suffering heavy casualties.

Parker found several men trapped by the incoming fire as he ran to give aid to those that had fallen. As soon as first aid was administered, Parker moved them over the ridge to relative safety.

While bandaging Bob Snyder's badly wounded leg, Parker's unit came under heavy machinegun fire that ripped through his parka, wounding him in the face for the second time. Snyder also suffered additional hits from the machine gun fire as well.

The Chinese attack grew with ferocity and causalities increased making their positions impossible to hold.

A determined navy corpsman, with an M-3 carbine warded off Chinese attackers as Parker defended and cared for his wounded comrades throughout the attacks.

Parker also suffered a painful leg wound as he worked on Sgt. Henry. The platoon's situation grew increasingly dire, and Parker began to gather the wounded marines ammunition and grenades.

As dawn broke, Charlie Company, 1st Battalion arrived to reinforce Parker's platoon. Welcomed airpower arrived to drive back the Chinese attack.

The platoons wounded were removed by Parker to the aid station for advanced treatment. He then joined corpsmen at Charlie Company's hospital to treat other wounded marines from the ridge.

Parker now joined the First Battalion as the unit fought its historic fourteen mile trek South from Yudam-ni to Hagaru. He also served as a pickup medic for a company of walking wounded as the 5th Regiment fought the rear guard action. The marines were walking out of the Chosin Reservoir; and one of the most verbal, if not the most famous marines, Lewis Berwell "Chesty" Puller noted as he stood on a rations box in a briefing tent: "I don't give a good goddamn how many Chinese laundrymen there are between us and Hungnam. There aren't enough in the world to stop a marine regiment going where it wants to go. Christ in his mercy will see us through." And so he did!

The battered US Navy Corpsman, Waller J. Parker, was flown from Hagaru-ri to Hungnam and on to a military hospital in Japan for treatment. He spent six weeks in

Yokosuka, Japan before being moved to Otsu, Japan for rest. He arrived in San Francisco on April 13, 1951.

The end of his war time tour was spent at the Alameda Naval Air Station in ward and pharmacy duties.

Waller James Parker was presented the NAVY CROSS; the second highest United States award for Valor by Admiral Waller. Corpsman Parker was also awarded a PURPLE HEART, PRESIDENTIAL UNIT CITATION and was eligible for the COMBAT ACTION RIBBON as well as other Korean campaign decorations.

A most memorable event occurred during a 12th Naval District inspection of our reserve unit.

As a young and inexperienced ensign of the inspection party passed in front of Chief Parker, he remarked "Chief, I know you must have some ribbons you could wear on that uniform. Make sure you do so on inspection night." As the tall and stoic Chief looked over the heads of the inspection party, he muttered a "Yes Sir."

The following month the cocky ensign reappeared with the inspection party. Much to my surprise the ensign had zero ribbons on his obviously new dress blue uniform.

As the party again passed the stoic Chief the inspection officer asked the ensign, "Ensign, do you recognize the ribbons on the chief's uniform."

The ensign mumbled what sounded like a "yes sir" as he stood eying the chief.

With a smirk on his face, the Senior Inspection Officer said "Well then, why don't you call them out in a loud and clear voice Ensign."

The ensign was able to mumble through "The Navy Cross and Purple Heart" when the Inspection Officer stopped him, and continued the inspection.

We were proud of our chief that night!

"Surfin the Yalu
Frostbite stoic few
The real wave brutal pounding
Hung ten from Chosin

-Scott Parker

THE DOGS OF WAR

By

Robert Fregeau

When we hear the term hero, most of us think in this day and age anyway, of the military man on the front lines of combat in Iraq or Afghanistan. Yes, these are the heroes of our time and deserve the recognition and respect of every American. But what of the heroes of yesterday? Heroes come in all shapes, sizes, ages and breeds. Yes, breeds. Before you condemn this story as a case of animal magnetism; well, in this case it may very well be; read it before you make the judgment call. Their acts can be as heroic as those of any two-legged warrior of today. In fact, it could be said some of the acknowledged heroes of today may not have been here if not for a four-legged hero of yesterday.

Let me take you back to one of the first wars fought by American troops on foreign soil. It was called "The war to end all wars," or World War One (WW I). It was on April 6, 1917 that the Congress of the United States declared war on Germany.

On the fields of Yale University in 1917 a "doughboy", a term whose lineage is as much in doubt as the hero you are soon to meet, met on the field of training at that learned institution of knowledge.

It was Private John Robert Conroy, a member of the 102nd Infantry, 26th Division United States Army who was training for an American Expeditionary Forces role in WW I in Europe. He found a young, four legged, bob-tailed Boston bull puppy in the fields of Yale University and named him "Stubby." The two immediately developed a close relationship and Stubby was also befriended by other members in the unit. Over the course of the war, Stubby was the pride of the 26th Division from New England, also referred to as "The Yankee Division" because most of its men were assigned to National Guard units from the New England area.

During the passing weeks at Yale where the army was in training, the white and brown spotted bob-tailed puppy was fed and nurtured by Conroy and the men in his company. Over time, Stubby came to understand the meaning of bugle calls, drill marching routines and amazingly learned to salute with his right paw over his right eyebrow. This was done on command or he would replicate the motions of the soldiers in formation. Upon learning of Stubby's presence and abilities, the unit commander allowed Private Conroy to keep him in camp.

Upon completion of their training in New Haven, Connecticut and with orders to deploy to Europe, Conroy was unwilling to give up ownership of Stubby. Rather than abandon his four-legged friend, he smuggled the animal both by truck and rail to the embarkation port of Newport News, Virginia.

Stubby was subsequently secreted aboard the battleship USS Minnesota (BB-22) with his master, where he was given shelter in the ships coal bin for the first twelve hours of the voyage. Finally, when Conroy felt it was safe that the ship would not return to port, he released the dog from its confines of the coal bin and he was taken on deck. Stubby immediately became all the rage with both the soldiers and the ship's crew.

It was during this crossing to France that Stubby was outfitted with a set of ID tags, commonly referred to as "Dog Tags" by military personnel. They were fashioned by an unnamed machinist mate aboard the Minnesota prior to docking at St. Nazaire, France.

Upon debarking at the port, Stubby was soon discovered by one of the regimental commanders. True to military protocol, when confronted, Stubby rendered a salute in his best form and after heartfelt negotiations; he was made the official mascot of the 26th Division.

Stubby and his unit reached their assigned position on the front lines on February 5, 1918. The weather was miserable; constant rain had turned the trenches into mudbaths. Sickness among the unit was rampant and movement along the lines was met with sniper fire, resulting in a high casualty rate.

The German army exposed the Americans to a new form of warfare, gas. The use of these chemicals caused everything from blindness to death. Stubby was not immune to this form of attack and suffered his first battlefield injury from a gas attack. This exposure made him highly sensitive to the vapors. In an early morning gas attack several weeks after returning to the unit from medical treatment, Stubby was credited for saving the lives of numerous soldiers who were sleeping by biting the soldiers' uniforms and barking loudly.

In an incident which brought Stubby international attention, he discovered a German spy making maps of the American positions. The spy ran from his position and was chased and taken to ground by this now, much larger and trained Boston B Terrier. Stubby then created a noisy ruckus which brought American soldiers to his position and they seized the spy as a prisoner of war. For his actions in the field, Stubby was officially promoted to the honorary rank of sergeant.

In a subsequent attack, Sergeant Stubby suffered a large amount of shrapnel to his chest and legs from a German grenade. He was rushed to an aid station where he received life-saving care and was then transferred to a recovery hospital for surgery and a full recovery. While at the hospital, Stubby provided morale to both wounded soldiers and staff. Upon healing from his wounds he was returned to the front lines.

Following the armistice in November, 1918 Sergeant Stubby was introduced to U.S. President Woodrow Wilson who was in Europe reviewing the troops. Prior to returning to America, Sergeant Stubby was awarded several war medals by the French government for his service. Stubby returned to the United States in 1919 where he was presented, among others, medals of his service to the nation. One of the medals was a special gold medal from the Humane Education Society which was presented by General John J. Pershing, General of the Armies.

His politics notwithstanding, Sergeant Stubby visited the White House twice subsequent to his retirement from active duty. He met with Presidents Harding and Coolidge; but a transcript of their conversations was not made available to this author. He was also given honorary membership in the YMCA.

In his retirement from the military, Stubby went on to be the mascot of the Georgetown Hoyas basketball team near Washington, DC. Sergeant Stubby lived out his years under the watchful assistance of his lifelong companion and mentor John R. Conroy. A veteran of seventeen battles during World War One, Sergeant Stubby passed away on March 16, 1926.

His likeness with all of his honorary medals is on display at the Smithsonian's National Museum of Natural History in Washington, DC.

"I still remember the refrain of one of the most popular barrack ballads of that day which proclaimed most proudly that 'old soldiers never die; they just fade away.'"— General Douglas McArthur in his (McArthur's) farewell address to the Congress of the United States in 1951.

PATRIOTS OF WWII

By

Jack Miller

There were many heroes during the Second World War. The best known was probably Audie Murphy. The entire United States learned of his exploits. There is no doubt he was a hero and patriot.

But the patriots of that war outnumbered the heroes. The majority of these patriots never left the United States and probably never left their home towns. In my opinion, these same home town patriots were the same people who never picked up a gun to defend their country.

On December 7, 1941 I was six and a half years old. I lived in Marquette, Michigan a small town by many standards, in the Upper Peninsula. My dad had served in the First World War and then joined the Michigan State Police. On Sunday mornings, my mom, dad and four older sisters encircled the radio and listened to the comics being read and then we almost always got in the state police car assigned to dad and drove around town. That Sunday morning was no different until about noon. We were in downtown Marquette at one of the two stop lights we had; this was the one near the post office. Another car pulled up alongside us and motioned for dad to roll down his window. He did and the other driver yelled "The Japs bombed Pearl Harbor" Dad, as many others I'm certain asked the same question. "Where is Pearl Harbor?" The other driver yelled back, "Hell Jack, I don't know."

Michigan State Police cars did not have any sort of radios in them so dad immediately drove home and we again encircled the radio only this time we were not listening to the half hour stories of "Jack Armstrong The All American Boy," or "Mister Keene, tracer of lost persons," or "The Green Hornet" and his faithful friend Kato, or the many others we normally would have. Instead, we listened to news reporters tell us about the destruction of our navy stationed in Hawaii.

The next day we listened to President Roosevelt announce that a state of war existed between the United States and Imperial Japan. Before December 7, we had been receiving news reports mostly through "Movietone News" in the theaters. We had watched reports of Hitler and his National Socialist Workers Party in Europe. We watched as his army took over country after country. But we were not going to get involved except to perhaps build some tanks and planes, guns and ammo and send it to England and Russia so they could fight their war. Suddenly it became our war. Men flocked to recruiting stations and enlisted. They were going to go kick some butt and end the war by the next Christmas.

With all the men enlisting, who was going to build the war equipment necessary for our soldiers? Who would run the farms, milk the cows? Who would refine the iron ore into steel, mine the copper, or even make gunpowder? That is where the patriots rose to the situation.

"Rosie the Riveter" was born. Newspaper collections were organized. Scrap metal was collected. Victory gardens were planted. Meatless Tuesdays and Fridays were followed. Civilian Defense volunteers walked neighborhoods looking for lights during blackouts. Most everyone, young and old, every loyal American became part of the war effort.

Rosie the Riveter became a symbol of what a woman could do. They built planes, tanks and automobiles. Work that had been exclusively male now was being done by females. They worked in mills and factories and, I'm certain that if asked, they would have gone into the mines digging ore and coal and copper.

Kids collected newspapers and tin cans. If a spring had fallen off a truck, before the driver could stop, it would be in some kids scrap iron pile, soon to be donated to the war effort.

Older men and women planted victory gardens. Some planted on their own unused property and some planted farms on donated property. Food grown was distributed to local residents with surplus going to feed the military.

Families knew that every Tuesday and Friday they would eat fish or macaroni and cheese for dinner. The meat was rationed with the majority going to feed the military who also celebrated meatless days.

Men who were too old to volunteer for a military branch of the service volunteered to be Air Raid Wardens. They were issued a tin helmet and an armband with the letters "CD" on them. It stood for civil defense. During blackouts in the early years of the war everyone had to turn out their lights so enemy airplanes wouldn't know where to bomb. If you got caught violating a blackout, then the wrath of the Civil Defense Force would befall you. When we had air raid drills, air raid wardens directed the people to the nearest shelter and then the wardens remained outside, exposed, to watch for enemy planes.

In retrospect, I feel much of this was paranoia on our part. We were too far away for any enemy aircraft to fly from Germany or Japan and attack us. Perhaps it was propaganda. But what it did was great. It made America into a cohesive group. Strong and determined to resist any attempt to force us to give up our form of government, our life style, and our freedoms.

I know as a six and a half year old kid and for the next four years I killed many Japanese and Germans soldiers with my play rifle and my squad of friends who felt the same. Young soldiers? Yes we were. Young patriots? We were that too, and proud to be so. Too poor to have a flag, too patriotic to not love what our flag stood for, and too rich with freedoms to have them taken away.

Yes, the United States had many patriots then. Are they still around? Yes, I believe they are. Perhaps they only need to be looked for, then recognized and thanked.

ONE OF THE PROUD, THE FEW

By

Robert M. Cawley

When we hear those words only one thought hits our minds ... the United States Marine Corps. There is no man whom fits that description better than Herbert Joseph Thomas, Jr. who was posthumously awarded the Congressional Medal Of Honor for his actions on November 7, 1943, at Koromokina River, Bougainville Island, Solomon Islands.

Herbert J. Thomas, Jr. was born in Columbus, Ohio, but spent the bulk of his childhood in South Charleston, West Virginia. He proved to be an outstanding high school football player and was awarded a football scholarship to Virginia Polytechnic Institute. In 1940 as a senior at VPI, he led his team in pass receptions and topped all Virginia college players in scoring. He was named to the Virginia Tech Sports Hall of Fame.

Thomas left VPI two months short of graduation to enlist in the Army Air Corps. Later he transferred to the Marines because so many of his friends were in the corps. He was soon a sergeant in the 1st Battalion, 3rd Marines.

In part, his citation for the battle on the Solomon Islands reads:

"Although many of his men were struck by enemy bullets as he led his squad through dense jungle undergrowth in the face of severe hostile machine-gun fire, Sgt. Thomas and his men fearlessly pressed forward into the center of the Japanese position and destroyed the crews of two machine guns by accurate rifle fire and grenades. Discovering a third gun more difficult to approach, Sgt. Thomas carefully placed his men closely around him in strategic positions from which they were to charge after he had thrown a grenade into the emplacement. When the grenade struck vines and fell back into the midst of the group, Sgt. Thomas deliberately flung himself upon it to smother the explosion, valiantly sacrificing life for his comrades."

Inspired by his selfless action, his men unhesitatingly charged the enemy machine-gun nest and with fierce determination, killed the crew and several other defenders.

In addition to the Congressional Medal of Honor, Sgt Thomas was posthumously awarded the Navy Cross, Bronze Star, Purple Heart, Presidential Unit Citation, and Asiatic-Pacific Campaign Medal. A Gearing Class Navy Destroyer, the "USS Herbert J. Thomas was named after him as was a hospital in South Charleston, West Virginia, plus a long highway bridge in the beautiful West Virginia hills. Initially buried in the U.S. Military Cemetery on Bougainville, his remains were reinterred in Sunset Memorial Park Cemetery in South Charleston.

Herbert Joseph Thomas, Jr., truly one of the proud, the few...Semper Fi!

THE FLAG ON THE MOUNTAIN

By

Keith Bettinger

There are things I enjoy seeing, things that make me happy that I live here in the United States of America. Seeing large American flags billowing in breezes can move me to tears. I love to see the changing colors of autumn leaves in the Northeast. I love watching ocean waves crashing on shores whether it be the Atlantic or the Pacific Ocean. Both are beautiful. I love to see the mountains in the Southwest as well as the Grand Canyon. When you see those mountains for the first time, your thoughts will immediately go to *America the Beautiful* and you will suddenly understand the lyrics proclaiming "Purple Mountains Majesty". The Grand Canyon too, is a sight to behold. It is a gift from God that has to be witnessed to be appreciated.

There are also special places in other parts of the country. I was to the top of World Trade Center on three different occasions and now cherish the memories of those trips. I have been to the Statue of Liberty and know she must have cried on September 11, 2001. I never tire of traveling to Washington, D.C. The monuments to our heroes and great buildings of our government stand before you and bring our great history to the forefront of our minds.

I made my first trip to Washington, D.C. in 1956. The history of my generation was only starting. I have a photo of me standing on the steps of the Lincoln Memorial. A short distance away is a very special place, the Viet Nam Memorial. On my first trip to Washington Viet Nam wasn't even yet a part of our history. Today it is the military event by which all current military events are compared.

Besides the Viet Nam Memorial my other favorite Memorials in Washington are the National Law Enforcement Officers Memorial, the Korean War Memorial and United States Marine Corps Memorial. This is the bronze sculptured statue of five marines and one navy corpsman raising the American Flag on Mount Suribachi on Iwo Jima. It stands just on the outskirts of Arlington Cemetery. This is a memorial that will grab your heart when you see our flag of red, white and blue waving and contemplate what it must have meant to all those marines and sailors who watched it being raised during some the most horrible combat of World War II. It will bring tears to your eyes if you fly to Reagan International Airport and are fortunate enough to pass over on your airplane's approach and see all the white gravestones of our veterans standing at attention row after row in Arlington Cemetery.

I am appalled when I see people revel in their own ignorance. Jay Leno, the television show host, goes on the street and asks people questions about our country's history. Their ignorance should embarrass them, but they laugh and giggle at their own stupidity and have no knowledge of why this country is great.

In 2002 I moved here to Las Vegas. I had to learn to find my way around a new community after more than fifty years on Long Island in New York. In my travels I took a freeway, the 215, and came to the intersection with Cheyenne Road. Like so much of the Las Vegas Valley it is an area of transition going from vacant beautiful desert to new homes in subdivisions. But there is something very special that stands out at this location. On the southwest corner is a mountain. Not a very big one as compared to other mountains, but a very special one. Since the first time I saw this mountain there has always been an American flag flying proudly from the top. I have seen it flying during all the seasons we experience here in the desert. I have seen it fly as a new flag and over time watched it become tattered in our desert winds. When that happens, soon thereafter, someone goes up to the top of the mountain and exchanges the worn veteran flag with a bright new flag to take its place. It is like the changing of the guard at the Tomb of the Unknown Soldier in Arlington Cemetery, but here at our mountain I have never seen the honors performed.

I don't know who these wonderful people are who take the time to maintain our country's flag on this solitary mountain. In fact, I don't think I want to know who they are. The mystery makes them and what they do more special because it is a selfless act of patriotism, an act of love for our great country and a gift to our citizens. I do know my heart skips a beat every time I see that flag. I know I slow down whenever I approach the mountain and look to see that the flag is still there. I also know I am happy to call Nevada my home, where some special people take the time, incur the expense and trek up the mountainside to make sure an American flag always stands proudly upon the top of that mountain beckoning to the citizens below.

SHOOTOUT

By

Dennis N. Griffin

The men and women of law enforcement don't have the luxury of picking and choosing each and every situation they become involved in. They respond to calls for service as dispatched, and react to what they observe while on the streets. Complaint-takers can reduce the risk to officers by obtaining detailed information of the situation the officer is responding to. And the officer's training, experience and instincts can guide him or her in how they handle the various circumstances they encounter while on patrol. But nothing is cast in stone. Every call and incident carries its own unique problems and dangers. Yet to keep us and our communities safe, these dedicated individuals are out there day after day putting their lives on the line.

One such person is Enrique Hernandez. Enrique is a cop in Las Vegas, Nevada, and in my eyes is a true hero.

In 2002, 28-year-old Las Vegas Metropolitan Police Department Officer Enrique Hernandez lived on the northwest side of Las Vegas with his wife Leean and their year-old daughter Maricela. The former marine had graduated from the police academy in June, and finished riding with a field-training officer that October. He was at the beginning of what appeared to be a promising law-enforcement career. But late that year he was involved in an incident that nearly took his life. I had an opportunity to interview Officer Hernandez in 2003.

It was December 12, and Officer Hernandez was working alone on patrol on the 3 p.m. to 1 a.m. shift. At about 10:20, he was stopped at a traffic light at the intersection of Eastern and Bonanza. Facing southbound on Eastern, he observed a dark-colored SUV turn from Bonanza onto Eastern, also heading south. The vehicle had no license plate, nor was any permit, sticker or decal visible. Immediately after making the turn, the SUV pulled into a gas station and convenience store located on the southeast corner of the intersection. As the traffic light changed, Officer Hernandez proceeded through the intersection and followed the suspect vehicle into the parking lot. He turned on his car's roof lights, planning to stop the vehicle and determine its registration status.

Although many police officers might argue that there is no such thing as a "routine" traffic stop, up until this point nothing had happened to cause Hernandez to become alarmed. There was no indication that there was anything particularly unusual or dangerous about the SUV. But unknown to Hernandez, its driver, 24-year-old Javier Duarte Chavez, was an illegal immigrant. Previously convicted of a felony in Nevada, Chavez had served time in the state prison system and been deported to Mexico upon his release. At that time, he'd been warned that he'd be in big trouble if he returned to the

United States. In spite of that, he did come back, using the alias of Saul Morales Garcia. He told family and friends that he would never again go to prison or be sent back across the border.

That wasn't Chavez' only problem. On this night he was driving back from the residence of a man and woman who owed him money and were refusing to pay. Though armed with a stolen .38 revolver, the slight, five-foot-tall Mexican, left the couple's home without the money after being told the police had been called.

It will never be known for sure whether Chavez thought the police were trying to stop him for the incident that had just occurred, although that seems like a strong possibility. Whatever was in his mind, he had no intention of letting Officer Hernandez get hold of him.

The lives of both men were drastically altered by the events of the next two minutes and forty-five seconds.

"I put my red lights on, but the SUV swung around out of the parking lot and headed back south on Eastern. I called in that I was in a pursuit and gave the direction of travel. The suspect made a left on Cedar, a right on 28th Street, and then a left on Marlin. He started out with a lead on me, but I was gaining on him all the time," Hernandez remembers.

"Shortly after we got on Marlin, he lost control of the vehicle, jumped the curb and hit a light pole. I pulled in to the curb behind him. He hit that pole pretty hard and I didn't think he'd get out and run right away, but he did. I called in that I was now in a foot pursuit and the chase was on again.

"We were running through an apartment complex and I was several yards behind. All of a sudden I saw one of the apartment doors open and he ran inside, the door shut behind him. He hadn't displayed a weapon yet, but it was obvious there was more to this than I had originally thought. In my mind, I was concerned that he may take the occupants of the apartment hostage. I drew my gun, opened the door, and went in. I didn't see the suspect, but there was a woman standing inside the door and a couple of little kids. The woman started screaming.

"It was a small apartment. The living room was on my right and I could see that the next room toward the back was a kitchen area, with a sliding glass door leading to the outside. I didn't know if the suspect had gone out the back or was somewhere in the apartment. I started moving cautiously toward the kitchen, stopping by the wall that separated the two rooms. As I again went forward into the kitchen, I detected movement against the wall to my left, about five feet away. Then I saw two muzzle flashes. My left arm was jerked back, but I didn't realize right away that I'd been hit. We then fired at each other simultaneously. I learned later that my round struck him near the right armpit and exited out his back. His bullet got me in my right forearm, my gun arm. It shattered the bone, then traveled up my arm and lodged in my shoulder; it's still in there. It felt like the arm had been blown off. It went dead and I lost the feeling in it; my gun fell out of my hand to the floor. I was now totally defenseless. It turned out that his wound wasn't debilitating."

There was a brief pause, during which Officer Hernandez realized that he had to get out of that apartment. As he started to retreat, he accidentally kicked his gun, knocking it under a piece of furniture. Before he could get out of the room, Chavez again opened fire. Hernandez was struck in his side, neck, and leg. He stumbled toward the front door, falling, then, regaining his feet. He made it outside and fell to the ground about ten feet from the door. Chavez, his gun now empty, fled in the other direction through the sliding-glass doors. It was later learned that the apartment in which the shooting occurred was where Chavez lived. The screaming woman was his girlfriend.

Hernandez continued his story, "A guy came out of the apartment and asked if I was okay and told me not to die. It turned out that he was the suspect's brother-in-law. He'd been upstairs taking a shower while the shooting was going on. I asked him to call 9-1-1 and tell them what had happened. The last they'd heard from me was when I called in the foot pursuit. Responding units would have no idea exactly where I was."

As additional personnel arrived, they administered medical treatment while Hernandez, who remained conscious at all times, provided suspect information. He said it wasn't until he got into the ambulance that the pain began to set in.

While the wounded officer was being transported to the hospital, his survival uncertain, the hunt for Javier Duarte Chavez began. SWAT and K-9 teams soon tracked the fugitive to a nearby row of unoccupied apartments. One of the dogs confirmed that Chavez was hiding in an airshaft a few feet above the floor. As SWAT officers prepared to enter the apartment, they were not certain of how much ammunition Chavez had for the .38, and thought he might have picked up Hernandez' service weapon, which remained undiscovered at the scene of the shooting.

After several unsuccessful attempts to get Chavez to surrender, he pointed his .38 at the officers and they opened fire, killing the suspect. It was later determined that his gun had been empty and the incident was a case of "suicide by cop." A coroner's inquest and Use of Force Board both ruled that the shooting of Chavez was justified.

Officer Hernandez was released from the hospital before Christmas, but he faced more than a year of therapy and rehabilitation. In January 2004 he completed treatment and was taken off medication. He returned to work on light-duty at the Downtown Area Command and the Public Information Office. In early March he was assigned to the Domestic Violence Detail on restricted duty. He carries a gun, but is prohibited from getting involved in physical altercations. It is anticipated that the three bullets still in his body will eventually work themselves out and no surgery is planned. "My right arm is in good shape. My hand is only about 60% and my left foot hurts most of the time, but I'm back to work and I'm happy," Enrique says. He has no complaints about how Metro has treated him since the shooting.

"I couldn't ask for anything more. My Metro family has done everything possible in the way of help and support," he said.

And finally, the big question. On that night, wounded and unarmed, did he think he was going to die?

"I never thought that. I knew I was going to live," Hernandez said confidently.

Under those circumstances, how could he be so sure?

"Because I wasn't going to let a guy like him kill me."

And he didn't.

A NATION OF BELIEF

By

Rena Winters

Blessed is the nation whose God is the Lord, and the people whom he hath chosen for his own inheritance.

Our country was founded on its belief in God, in the summer of 1776, delegates from thirteen colonies met to consider the future of their new country. Suggestion after suggestion was offered and rejected. Finally the discouraged delegates turned to Benjamin Franklin for his opinion. Hesitating a moment he slowly rose and delivered a brief but powerful message based on Psalm 127 "Except the Lord build the house, they labor in vain, except the Lord keep the city, the watchman waketh but in vain." He suggested a time of prayer. A spirit of unity resulted and the declaration of independence was written. As the liberty bell range for the first time in Independence Hall, it proclaimed the birth of the United States of America on July 4, 1776.

Eighty-seven years after 1776, during a time of great crisis President Lincoln in his famous Gettysburg address, challenged the people of America to resolve "That this nation, under God, shall have a new birth of freedom - and that government of the people, by the people, for the people shall not perish from the earth." There are forces at work today which are trying to take away this freedom. These enemies are strong. Unless America acknowledges her dependence on God, we could lose this freedom that's so dear to us.

Prayer has changed the course of history in the past. It is still as powerful today. "If my people, which are called by my name, shall humble themselves, and pray, and seek my face, and turn from their wicked ways. Then will I hear from heaven, and will forgive their sin, and will heal their land."

The late President Kennedy, in his inaugural address, said "Do not ask what your country can do for you, but ask what you can do for your country." Pray, pray that our United States of American may continue as a nation under God.

In any election year, I beseech you to thoroughly understand what the candidates' platforms are. Seek the truth, do not be misled. Ask questions. Do they believe in God? Will they stand up for America during items of tribulation? Are their beliefs and yours cohesive? These are the people that will represent you. Are they truly your choice?

Take time out of your busy schedule and study the issues, know your candidates. Most of all get out and vote when the time comes. Too many Americans suffer from apathy. They refuse to take the responsibility of what has happened to our country. It's our fault. It's our country, yours and mine. It is time that we face the problems instead of ignoring them. They will not go away. They are only becoming worse.

Why did we vote to take prayer out of the schools? Were we afraid that it would poison our children, or did it come about because we suffered from apathy and just did not respond. This is one small example of what can happen if we are sleeping. Our country will not be taken over from outside, but from within. Failure to recognize the insidious workings of a different doctrine will allow it to grow and spread and become acceptable, even fashionable.

Why should publicly lighted crosses be forced to be taken down because a few people find it disagreeable? Why should the nativity scenes be taken from city and government property at Christmas time because it offends someone? This is a free country and each of us has the right of self expression. When we take away these rights we are limiting our power.

Today the greatest need of our country is prayer. It is also the greatest need of national and world leaders today. As we recognize the seriousness of these times, we need to turn to God in intercessory prayer.

How often the past events of history have been changed because of prayer. Prayer is of primary importance. We are reminded to pray for all men everywhere. I have read, that if we pray for one country each day, we would pray for the entire world three times in one year. To us the Christian God has given the privilege of praying. Our country desperately needs our intercession in these days. May we join hearts in prayer for our beloved United States of America, and for her people no matter where they are, or what they are, or who they are.

May God Bless America.

AMONGST THE SHADOWS AND STONES

By

Keith Bettinger

I don't know if my feelings and priorities about Memorial Day were different that year because the holiday fell on May 30, as it used to in the past. Maybe, it was the impending calendar change to the new millennium. It might have been that my own fiftieth birthday was approaching, arriving right after the millennium change. That could have made me more reflective as I approached my own half century. It also could have been that during the previous year, I saw the movie **Saving Private Ryan**. When I walked out of the theater, I was emotionally exhausted. I came away saying, *"Every politician should have to watch this film, before he can vote to send someone else's child off to war."* Maybe my observations were distorted when I looked at Viet Nam veterans. I thought to myself how old they appeared to be, and suddenly, I realized these are the American heroes of my generation. I do know that my father and my uncle are both veterans. They entered the service near the end of World War II, and my uncle is now in his 80s; my father recently passed away at 80. The other veterans from World War II are older and it just seems that all the sacrifices of their generation are being forgotten as time passes all of us by.

My wife and I talked before that holiday weekend. We decided we would make that Memorial Day like the ones we remembered when we were children, the holiday when veterans weren't so old, they marched in parades and honored all of those who served. The Memorial Days we remembered had stores that closed on that special holiday. We decided we wanted an old-fashioned Memorial Day. We would honor and remember our veterans.

To celebrate that Memorial Day, I decided to do a number of things that would be different. I organized members of one of the police organizations to which I belong. We placed flags at the graves of our veterans and their families at *Long Island National Cemetery*. We did it on Saturday, May 29. We walked amongst the gravestones. Each one had a name. They all cast shadows. The stones cast the shadows now, as the people they represent did, when they walked amongst us.

As we walked amongst the gravestones, we read names, we read dates, and sometimes we had our hearts broken. We saw the names of veterans laid to rest after they had fought in World War I, the Great War; the war that was supposed to end all wars. We saw stones for veterans of World War II, the Korean War, the Viet Nam War, and even the Spanish American War. We saw the names of spouses of veterans. Sometimes they were alone. Sometimes husbands and wives were joined together for eternity. Our hearts were broken as we read "Child of -" or simply "infant". We saw aging veterans remembering their friends. They bowed their heads in a moment of silent prayer and reflection, and then they placed an American flag at a special gravestone. There were *Cub Scouts* and *Brownies* running amongst the stones, placing flags at each one - the next generation of Americans was showing their thanks.

It was nice to be able to reflect on all that was done for this country by the heroes with whom we spent time. There was a special feeling amongst those that decorated the graves. It brought out such strong emotions. They would be back again the following year, walking amongst the shadows, placing a flag at each stone.

On Memorial Day, my wife and I went to visit Long Island National Cemetery, because our family and friends are there. Along the way, we stopped and purchased fresh flowers. It was time for us to pay our respects to some special individuals.

The first stop was my wife's parents grave. They are together. My wife's father fought in World War II. He served in North Africa and Europe. I never had the opportunity to meet him, he was gone before my wife and I met. I did enjoy knowing my mother-in-law and I do miss her. We always visit their grave on holidays and birthdays. However, that day we stopped to say thank you for what my wife's father did when it meant so much. We also had to thank her mother, for all she sacrificed while he was overseas for years. If not for them and the others like them, we would not be as blessed as we are today.

The next stop was the grave of the parents of a retired police officer from California. His father died when he was a small child. His father was serving in North Africa at the time, and died in combat. Eventually he was brought home and interred on Long Island. The retired police officer never knew his father. He was left with the stories his mother shared with the family for the rest of her life. She moved her children from New York to California, to make a better life. Her husband sacrificed his life for his country. His wife sacrificed to raise a wonderful family. She never forgot him. She never remarried. In 1994, after she died, she was returned to Long Island and was interred with her husband. I sometimes wonder if maybe, somewhere, while fighting in the deserts of North Africa, my wife's father and this police officer's father might have met.

The final stop was to see my friend Bill. We met the day we were sworn into the police department. Bill was a Viet Nam veteran who died of leukemia. Until that Memorial Day, I never knew his middle name was Walter. I didn't know he was born in 1947, almost three years older than me. I know he had a beautiful wife and a wonderful daughter and son. They made his eyes light up whenever he spoke about them. I know they miss him; there were flowers from a previous visit, at his grave. I know he was taken from us too soon, in 1988, when he was only 41. It seems like such a short time ago, that I was standing in a police honor guard, saying good-bye to my friend. I know he was a gentle soul and a good friend. He was there for me when I needed his friendship. He was also there for an elderly couple in his patrol sector. They were destitute, and Christmas was rapidly approaching. The old couple had a nice Christmas because Bill filled their home oil tank with heating oil. He bought them food, a Christmas tree and presents to make their holiday special. He was a kind hearted and fun loving soul.

He was a person I am glad I knew. I know you would have liked him, he was special. When he was 26, I saw him being teased by his brother. His father was listening and gave him one of those fatherly looks with raised eyebrows. Bill just looked at him and said, "Oh Daddy!" You have to like a man who fought in a war, worked the streets as a cop, and could still call his father Daddy. I wish my wife had met Bill, but it never happened. I am glad she went with me on Memorial Day. She made the visit easier, with that special look she gave me as she held my hand. It let me know she understood.

History has many sad commentaries. In the early 1960s, General MacArthur went back to the Philippines where he was greeted by cheering crowds. A young high school girl presented him with a bouquet of flowers, and welcomed him to the Philippines. She then asked a question that was filled with irony, "Have you been here before?" With all that he and his troops had done, he was forgotten by the generation he fought so hard to keep safe.

I am glad my wife and I decided to spend part of our day the way we did. Our veterans, alive or dead, are heroes to be thanked for all that they have done. They cannot be forgotten. I am glad I got to spend part of my weekend with some of them, amongst the shadows and the stones.

AN EARLY HERO

By

Charles McKee

When the coal mine just outside of Raton, New Mexico exploded in July, 1944 it not only killed my grandfather and five other miners, it reversed the direction of our family.

One of my father's best friends and workmates was now dead. Mining had lost it flavor for our family, and my grandmother seemed in a deep slump following my grandfather's death.

My father left Raton, and relocated in Richmond, California. The only answer for the move was "There are war jobs there." My father had already been discharged from the US Army about five years prior. He had a wife and new child to support. He secured a job with the Santa Fe Railroad and then Standard Oil in Richmond.

Within three months after we arrived in Richmond it was during one of the worst rain storms to hit the bay area. We cannot describe the condition we were in when my father met our train at the Santa Fe Depot, at the foot of MacDonald Avenue.

We lived in what would be called a ghetto by today's standards, and I seemed to know that my parents had little extra money to spend.

Our family used the ferry rides from Richmond to the cross bay city of San Rafael, as a family outing.

I marveled at the military and civilian marine traffic as we crossed the bay; as I had developed a love of ships and the sea as soon as we arrived on the West Coast. World War II was in full swing and war industry abounded throughout the Richmond-Oakland areas.

Washington grammar school, in Point Richmond, was within two blocks of Kaiser's ship yard number three. And my Mother had found work at Lucky Stores in front of the shipyards.

This could not have worked out better if I had planned it. And, plan it I did. It was just a short walk down Cutting Boulevard to the inside nose of the first building dock. Security at this location was non-existent, and that made it easy for me to watch ships for three hours.

The school missed me just ten minutes after school started, but, they had no clue where I might have gone. Foot traffic was very heavy in the area but they still could not find me.

As I sat on a large rock, I heard a voice behind me say "How about some ice crème?" He had found me. Hans Toft, dressed in the uniform of the Richmond Police Department. *Wow, what a nice policeman and ice crème too.*

My Mother's absence from work during child searching did not set well with her even though I was having a good time.

I had fond memories of the officer who saved me that day by the bay. But alas, my escapes were curtailed when we moved some twenty- five blocks away to another war housing complex. I would not see the officer for quite some years after the war ended.

Some twenty-five years later, and just five miles from our first meeting; I again met the hero in blue.

We were both in uniform; mine a Deputy Sheriff, and his; a Department of Defense Security Officer.

The man sipping coffee at the outside standup counter of the hamburger stand looked strangely familiar. As I walked back to my patrol car I noticed his name tag, "Hans Toft."

We chatted for a short time, and I was amazed that he had remembered the circumstances surrounding my escape, and how he had found me that morning in 1945.

This hero had left some very good memories with me. Even though we promised to meet again for coffee in the same place, I never saw Officer Hans Toft again.

NOT ALL HEROES GET MEDALS

By

Jack Miller

In my time, I have seen World War Two, the Korean Conflict, called a police action, the Viet Nam War, another police action, Operation Desert Storm and now the Global War on Terror. During a portion of this same time American men were drafted into service. It did not matter if you wanted to go or not. If drafted you went, or you became a criminal and could be prosecuted and sent to prison. The draft ended in 1973, however all males over the age of eighteen must still register for the draft in the event a war is declared and there are not enough volunteers. Today all our military services are made up of volunteers. They are there because they want to serve.

During the periods of declared war and authorized police actions, men and women in the service, drafted or not, performed heroically. Some have been recognized for their performance of duty by being awarded medals for their actions.

Purple Hearts are awarded to those men and women wounded in combat.

Bronze stars are awarded for bravery and other notable action.

Silver Stars are awarded for gallantry in action.

Military Service Crosses may be awarded for extraordinary heroism.

Medals of Honor, our highest and most esteemed medal is awarded for heroism above and beyond the call of duty.

There are also decorations designated for personnel who served in a particular area or during a particular time or who have performed admirably.

But there were other men and women who answered the call to duty, performed honorably and some heroically, who completed their term of service but received no medals. Yet, without them, many designated heroes would not have received medals or have been recognized. They are the forgotten heroes.

This is not meant to devalue, in any form, the men and women recognized as heroes. They deserved to be honored and their stories told for years to come. They are what make this country great. Their attitude alone is worthy of news' articles, movies, television shows, even speeches about them. My point is that they were selected to be recognized to receive medals. What about those others who performed heroically but were not selected? What about those who merely performed their duty but were not recognized for it? What about those heroes who did not get a medal?

Let us take a simple case of the award of the Purple Heart. A soldier gets wounded. The wound is easily seen. He is carried by litter to a jeep. He is driven to a first aid station where his wound is dressed. If it is severe enough, he is sent by ambulance to an airfield, then carried by aircraft to a hospital where he is treated so he can either be returned to duty or sent back home for rehabilitation. Along the way an officer comes along and pins the Purple Heart medal to his pillow. The soldiers who carried the litter, drove the jeep, the doctors, nurses or corpsmen that treated him along the way are not recognized. Nor is the ambulance driver, the aircrew, or the hospital staff given medals for their heroics, even though they performed their duty honorably. It does not detract from the award of the Purple Heart, but without them the soldier receiving it would have probably died on the battle field.

Certainly, those who have been honored for their service with the award of medals should be honored. They performed as others think they will, or want to perform, under grave circumstances. I believe all men and women, all American men and women who have been raised in the climate of God and country, ask themselves what they would do in a dangerous situation. Would they run into a burning building to save someone? Would they stand under a window and try to catch a falling baby? Would they rush to help a person injured and bleeding even though they don't know the person? I think we all have had such thoughts similar to these.

But fortunately or unfortunately, we all have not had the opportunity to prove to ourselves what we really would do in those circumstances. Medals are not awarded for what might have been.

During my past military career, I have been surrounded by military men and women, some of whom had been selected to be recognized for their actions. I am proud to have known every one of them. I am also proud to know those who also served honorably, but who did not receive any medals.

Specifically, the unrecognized heroes of the Cold War are the people I am referring to. They were the men and women who stood posts guarding the borders of our country and responsible for giving the alarm. More often than not these posts were on mountain tops, isolated from civilization, scant creature comforts like theaters, restaurants, schools, parks and the like. In most cases weather was also an enemy with wind, rain, snow, cold, and heat being their constant companion. These were the Air Force Radar Site operators, the Army personnel who manned missile battalions, the Navy and Coast Guard boat crews, and the Marines at their varied posts. Men and women away from their homes, their loved ones, their families and even civilization because they were ordered by their government to be away. These are the unsung heroes who I believe should be recognized with a specific medal.

There should be a Cold War Service Medal approved by Congress and awarded by our government. Presently the only official recognition they receive, if they apply for it, is a Certificate of Recognition. A Cold War Service medal should be awarded to honor their service, and the fact that during the Cold War we were not attacked. In my book that means they did their jobs above and beyond the call of duty.

ON PATRIOTISM

By

Marshal Taylor

Patriot: One who loves and defends his or her country; a person who loves, supports, and defends his or her country and its interests with devotion.

Synonyms: lover of his country, good citizen, statesman, nationalist, volunteer, loyalist, jingoist, chauvinist.[1]

Zealot: A fervent and even militant proponent of something.

Synonyms: crusader, fanatic, ideologue (*also* idealogue), militant, partisan (*also* partizan), red hot, true believer. **[2]

Everyone seems to know what patriotism is, since the word gets tossed around so much these days. But the problem with patriotism is that it can be a good thing as well as a bad thing. For instance, a patriotic young Nazi might have joined the Wehrmacht and answered his nation's call to fight for the Aryan people; was he a patriot? He would have been

---

[1] Webster's New World Roget's A-Z Thesaurus
[2] Merriam-Webster dictionary

supporting his country's desire for dominance and lebensraum, so he was, in that sense, a patriot. We might react queasily to this example because we can look back and see the evil done in the name of patriotism.

Obviously, it's not enough to love your country and to try to serve it, there needs to be more – there has to be an engagement of thought, or else the benevolent wish to do something for the country can become a nightmare. After all, the most common defense at the Nuremburg trials was "I was following orders." In other words, the defendants gave up their ability to think and blindly followed someone else's ideas of what was right.

Patriotism, divorced from reason easily becomes zealotry, and the patriot who does not examine what he or she is supporting becomes a partisan. A patriot must look at things, do some critical thinking, and then be able to clearly state what he or she believes in.

To approach a considered or deliberate patriotism means to have some basic understanding of what one's country - our country in this example - stands for. As Americans, considered or deliberate patriotism means understanding the Constitution, Bill of Rights, and the principles of our government; not necessarily to be able to quote these works by heart, but to just understand them.

It's hard work to be a true patriot, and simply waving a flag, putting a pin in a lapel, and joining a militia group does not automatically make one a patriot. To paraphrase Socrates, who said "the unexamined life is not worth living for a human being,"[3] The unexamined life is not truly patriotic.

---

[3] Plato, *Apologia 3a*

SCARS OF THE HEART

By

Keith Bettinger

Many a cop has said that police work is hours of boredom followed by moments of sheer terror. It can also be followed by years of physical and emotional pains as well as physical and emotional scars that never heal. Ron Corbin is not only this type of police officer, but one of the strongest and bravest you will ever meet.

Ron served two tours in Viet Nam as a US Army helicopter pilot. He never turned down a mission that was assigned to him. Although he was never wounded, he lost 27 friends whose names are posted on the Viet Nam Memorial in Washington, D. C.

When he was discharged he tested for and was accepted by the Los Angeles Police Department. After doing time in the street he was accepted onto the department's aviation unit. He quickly rose to be an instructor pilot for the department and lobbied for better equipment for the air crews, including fireproof flight suits and safety helmets.

On June 11, 1976, Ron and his partner, Student Pilot – Air Observer Jeffrey Lindenberg, prepared for a training flight in a Bell 47G-5 helicopter, the model you see in the television show MASH. They did a pre-flight safety inspection of the aircraft and prepared for takeoff.

Jeff flew the aircraft and they were airborne over Los Angeles. A short distance from the airport, near the large white Hollywood sign on top of the Hollywood Hills above the Los Angeles Zoo, just east of the Griffith Observatory, they had a catastrophic mechanical failure while practicing a landing approach. They had no time or altitude to auto-rotate down to a landing pad on top of the mountain. One of the landing skids on the helicopter came down on the cement landing pad as it was supposed to. The other skid did not clear the cement. It hit the pad and sent the helicopter careening 162 feet down the side of the mountain in a ball of flames created by the exploding fuel tanks consuming their full load of fuel.

Two hikers removed Ron's badly burned body from the burning helicopter. His non fire retardant suit had burned into his body and his eye protection melted over his eyes onto his face. Jeff could not be seen in the wreckage where he had become trapped by the flaming fuel tank. A Los Angeles Fire Department helicopter transported Ron to the hospital where he was treated for burns over 70 percent of body, 62 percent of the burns being second and third degree burns. People wondered would Ron survive the injuries, and if he did, would he survive the psychological aftermath. This was the start of the many types of pain he would have to endure for years to come.

At the hospital, the attending physician asked Ron's wife Kathy if she was going to stay. When she said she would stay at the hospital, the doctor clarified his question with another; are you going to stay in the marriage?

Her response was, "I love him. Of course I'm going to stay."

The doctor informed Kathy that many spouses can't deal with the trauma of burns and leave. Her statement set the course of treatment both physically and psychologically.

Although Ron knew deep down that Jeff could not have survived the crash, it was still a devastating shock and pain to be told that Jeff was dead. What hurts more is years of survivor guilt. Why Jeff and not me? He has a wife and a baby daughter. Could I have done something different? The answer is always no, but a survivor will continue to ask the question over and over again looking for the answer he wants to hear.

Many times a survivor doesn't understand that talking about the incident is a way of closing the incident. Explaining to others that one did all he could, helps the survivor realize he is correct, even though the outcome remains the same. Ron wanted to tell Lesa, Jeff's wife that Jeff did nothing wrong to cause the accident. Ron wanted to let her know that he too did everything he could do to avert the disaster. It simply was beyond anything humanly possible to prevent the disaster or change its outcome.

Lesa had more than she could handle at the moment. Jeff was dead. She was a widow. She had an infant daughter to raise alone. She had to deal with the department, the pension board, the press and an aching heart. She could not be part of Ron's recovery. She had to struggle with her own. The rebuff hurt. It was hard to understand from Ron's point of view, but understandable if you're a new widow.

Every department has strange retirement procedures. As badly injured and scarred as Ron was, it took three trips to the pension board during the course of five years to decide that Ron's career as a police officer was over. All he asked of Workers Compensation was free medical treatment for life to deal with his injuries and future complications. They agreed. But, when he learned he needed treatment for spinal injuries received in the crash, he found out that yes he did have free medical treatment for life, if the treatment was related only to burns. He was on his own for spinal problems.

Although physically limited, Ron continued to work. He never gave up on being a provider for his family. After retirement he continued his education, receiving degrees in interesting curriculums; a BA in Child Development, an MS in Elementary Education, and a PhD in Security Administration. It took a lot of courage to go back to school as an "old timer," a thirty year old, compared to students recently out of high school. It also took a lot of courage to wear a JOBST burn suit to class, scars showing, being constantly in pain and being stared at by the campus population. However, Ron finished his education and achieved the goals he set for himself.

Ron eventually moved to Las Vegas, NV. He went to work as a civilian crime prevention specialist for the Las Vegas Metropolitan Police Department. Later he became training manager for the police academy, a job in which he excels. He also never gave up the hope of eventually talking to Lesa about that night.

After the 9/11 attacks on this country, Las Vegas Police Sergeant Randy Sutton requested story submissions from police officers for a book – True Blue. The profit from the sales would go to the families of the police officers killed in the devastating attacks.

Ron had a story to share, not only with the readers but with Lesa. He wrote an open letter to Lesa, but instead of mailing it to her he published it in the book. Offers were made to deliver the letter to Lesa, but Ron declined the offer; if Lesa was to read the letter, somehow Lesa and the story would come together.

If you at home have Google or other search engines, it's fun to run your name through and see where it comes up. Lesa was on such an expedition playing on the computer. Lo and behold, her name and Jeff's appeared on the screen connected to the book – True Blue and Ron's open letter to Lesa.

Divine intervention had finally taken place. After reading the letter, Lesa was now ready to meet and talk to Ron. Time does not heal all wounds, but it helps ease some of the pain. After thirty-three years the two of them met and talked and talked and talked.

The next time they met, Kathy also met Lesa. They too talked and a sense of healing was happening for everyone. After all, healing is a family affair. Lesa's daughter Tina, now a young woman, met Ron and asked questions about the father she never knew. She read the story in True Blue and wanted a copy of the book, but it was not available. Ron gave her one of his copies. She in turn gave the book as a gift on Father's Day to her stepfather, the only father she really ever knew, also a Los Angeles Police Officer.

The psychological healing for Ron began and continues today. But it will never be a complete healing of the physical injuries. His skin feels sizes too small for his body when the scars constrict. It's kind of like trying to put a size eleven foot into a size nine shoe. Keeping scars moist is difficult when you live in the desert. Internal organs are overworked from years of trying to clear the body of toxins breathed in or absorbed through burnt tissues. It certainly takes a toll on a person victimized by fate and mechanics so many years ago, but, it doesn't slow Ron down. He smiles and laughs when he talks to you. He has a twinkle in his eyes when he shows photos of his lovely wife Kathy, his handsome sons, Jeff and Steve, and his beautiful daughter, Kim. He works hard to make sure that new recruits learn not only how to be police officers, but how to survive as police officers.

Ron no longer looks to the past with questions. He looks to the future with answers for himself and others.

TEARS OF THE HEART

By

Keith Bettinger

A wife watches her police officer husband leave for work every day. During four years of marriage this was an everyday occurrence for Lesa and Jeff Lindenberg. Lesa was thrilled when Jeff was accepted and assigned to the Los Angeles Police Department Air Support Division and no longer patrolled the streets of Newton Division, known to officers as "Shootin' Newton".

Jeff was happy to be teamed with pilot, Ron Corbin, a former U.S. Army, Viet Nam helicopter pilot. Jeff admired Ron's professionalism in such a specialized unit that normally runs on testosterone and often gets bogged down in bureaucracy. Ron was a respected and dependable instructor pilot. He also had a softer side that impressed Jeff. Jeff was struck by the fact that Ron carried a Bible in his briefcase at work.

The men carpooled to work. They were partners. They were a team. Their friendship grew and Jeff and Lesa were invited on occasion to the Corbin home for dinner. But the friendship that these two couples hoped to attain together was not to be. Fate would intervene before this could happen.

June 11, 1976 started like any other work day. Jeff and Ron were working and Lesa was home caring for their seven month old daughter, Tina. While taking care of Tina and working around the house, Lesa heard a heart wrenching radio news bulletin that a Los Angeles Police helicopter had crashed on a mountainside a few miles from the Hollywood sign in Griffith Park.

Lesa knew what that meant. Something inside her told her. She picked up Tina and ran through the backyard gate linking the two homes to her best friend's house. The friend's husband was a Los Angeles police officer too. He immediately started making phone calls and was told by officers at the Air Support Division to keep Lesa at his home. He was told the Captain was on his way to see her. Lesa worked for the police department too and knew its procedures and protocols. The arrival of a captain after an incident meant only one thing; he was responding to make a death notification.

The Captain told Lesa Jeff had died in the crash and fire as the helicopter fell 162 feet down the mountainside. Even though she was overwhelmed and had suddenly gone from wife and mother to widow and single mother all within one morning, she still found the strength to go to the hospital that night to comfort Kathy Corbin, Ron's wife, and to check on Ron's condition.

For weeks Lesa continued to receive support from the department, Jeff's friends and family members. But, as all survivors know, the support fades over time. People, who were there for you, soon return to their own busy lives. Some distance themselves because they don't know what to say or do. Meanwhile, the surviving family struggles all alone. At the time of Jeff's death there was no departmental support group for survivors. Police departments weren't as knowledgeable regarding the physical and psychological needs of the survivors in the past as they are now.

While struggling in that "all alone" stage, Lesa started to hear rumors about the crash, what caused it, and who was responsible for the tragedy. Misinformation took center stage and led to a need for answers. Lesa went to the scene of the crash, but the answers she needed weren't there. She read everything she could find regarding the crash and listened to comments made by pilots from Air Support Division. Lesa's mistake was taking these comments as gospel.

Four to five months after the crash, Lesa received a letter from Ron who was recovering from his injuries. He invited her and Tina to dinner at his home, but Lesa did not go. She couldn't go; she needed distance between herself and Ron. Ron sent her another letter later on, offering to answer any questions she had regarding the crash and to explain in detail what happened that day.

But Lesa couldn't see through the pain of her loss. With the misinformation that she received, and an emotional need for Jeff not to be at fault, which he wasn't, led to her blaming the only other person who could be responsible — Ron, the instructor pilot, the man to whom she entrusted her husband. She needed space to grieve and couldn't associate with Ron. In her mind, with the volumes of misinformation she had received, Ron was responsible, and that gave her a state of mind she could deal with; Jeff was a victim just like her. She never thought of Ron as a bad person, but she needed him as the focal point for her anger. Her survivor guilt was misdirected.

Lesa did worry about Ron and checked on him from time to time, but always quietly from behind the scenes. She continued to keep her distance. This was her survival technique.

As time passed a couple of Lesa and Jeff's friends stayed close to Lesa. They stopped by from time to time and made sure all the necessary departmental forms were filled out and processed for Lesa and Tina, and that they were receiving all the benefits they were entitled to receive. One of these friends was a fellow Los Angeles police officer named Charlie Manzo. On one visit he asked Lesa if Jeff's personal effects were ever returned. Lesa hadn't thought about it before. She asked if she could have Jeff's badge and his wedding ring.

Charlie made inquiries about Jeff's effects. The badge was gone. It had melted in the fire that had consumed him and the helicopter. However, once again by divine intervention, Jeff's wedding ring was returned to Lesa in perfect condition. It was a special gift that she needed to begin her healing process.

Lesa and Charlie developed a special friendship. Charlie's friendship was very special because he would let Lesa talk about Jeff and listened to her as she poured her heart out. This was something that Lesa needed. A couple of years later, their friendship grew, they fell in love and Lesa and Charlie married. They started a blended family that eventually led to a remake of the movie, **Yours, Mine and Ours,** with the arrival of their daughter Tracy. They've now been married over thirty years.

As the years went by 2009 came to be, and computers became household items. One day while Lesa was watching a television show, she heard a show guest talking about running your own name through the search engine **Google** and seeing what comes up. As a lark Lesa went to the computer and did just that. She was shocked to find her and Jeff's names connected to an article in the book **True Blue**. The story in the book was *Your Husband—My Partner - A letter to Lesa*. It was written by Ron in 2002, twenty-six years after the accident, and it was an open letter to Lesa. The letter told Lesa that Ron suffered from Survivor's Guilt as she did. He missed his partner, Jeff, every day and admitted he felt hurt when he was turned away by Lesa. Her pain caused him to hurt all the more. Lesa realized she was not alone in her grief. Ron too had suffered all these years. They both suffered from their own survivor's guilt.

After reading this emotional letter on the computer, Lesa felt compelled to reach out to Ron. She searched the police department's retiree directory for Ron's address. She read that he had relocated to Las Vegas, NV. She sent Ron a letter and told him she and Tina were traveling to Las Vegas for a family birthday celebration and she would like to meet with him. However, she was panicking a little after mailing the letter. She was afraid to contact him after she had avoided him for so many years. She put the letter in the mailbox and thought over and over again about removing it from the mailbox. However, divine intervention intervened again, and for the first time, the mailman arrived early and picked up the letter. Lesa was now committed.

A few days later she received an e-mail from Ron saying that he was looking forward to seeing her and Tina in Las Vegas. Lesa replied that she and Tina would be at the Monte Carlo Hotel and Casino and Ron could meet them there.

As Lesa sat in the hotel lobby awaiting Ron's arrival, she was panicking. Could she go through with it? She got up and was ready to leave, but when she turned around, standing there before her was Ron with two red roses in his hand, one for Lesa and one for Tina. Thirty-three years of heartfelt pain was eased as he told her to ask any question that needed an answer after all the years.

Lesa had many questions, and after suffering from misinformation overload for so many years, she finally found out that there was nothing Jeff or Ron could have done to prevent the crash. It was due to engine failure. All the "Monday Morning Quarterbacks" were proven wrong simply by asking Ron about the events of that day.

Lesa was upset with herself for not reaching out to Ron earlier. He had the answers he needed to share with her; the answers she so desperately needed to hear. She felt terrible that Ron had suffered from survivor guilt for so many years, and that she had not reached out to him sooner. After all, Ron was the last person to have been with her husband before he died.

Lesa and Ron share shattered dreams. Ron's career as a police helicopter pilot ended with his disability retirement. After two tours in Viet Nam flying helicopters and then the horrific crash, Ron's wife Kathy, asked him to give up flying. She too experienced the difficulties of being a survivor. Over the next 14 years, Kathy watched Ron every time a helicopter flew by. She realized he had never lost his love of flying. One day she looked at him and said, "Go ahead and fly if you want to. I'll be okay with it". At first Ron declined, but with Kathy's coaxing, he returned to recreational flying at a small airport in Southern California. He rented a small helicopter from time to time to fly family and friends on pleasure rides, like the rest of us do in our cars. Kathy went flying with Ron a few times, but between her white knuckles and hyperventilating, he knew she did not share in his love of flying. Soon after, he gave up flying.

Lesa's dream of growing old with Jeff and raising their family together came to a sudden end that tragic day. It doesn't mean that she doesn't love Charlie and their family, she does. But there is always a special place in one's heart for a first love. Tragedy broke the heart that held that special love on June 11, 1976.

Even though it's been so many years since the accident, grief knows no time boundaries. To this day, Lesa still has some difficulties just like many other survivors. She wonders if she dealt with her grief in the proper way. She has a love-hate relationship with helicopters. She enjoys seeing most of them, but stress sets in when they make low passes. She also can't stand to see the type of helicopter that Jeff died in. Griffith Park may be a tourist attraction and picnic area in Los Angeles, but it isn't a place to visit for Lesa. The Hollywood sign on the mountain near the crash site doesn't bother her, but water tanks on top of mountains, like the one near where Jeff and Ron crashed, make her remember that terrible day. She is still angry for listening to the people who gave her misinformation about the crash. Lesa tries to avoid June 11th each year.

Anniversary dates tend to have strange effects on many survivors. Something that gives Lesa a sense of peace on each June 11th anniversary date are the emails from Ron, letting her know he is thinking of her and Tina, and especially Jeff.

With this new found strength and ability to grow through her past anger Lesa has a positive outlook on life. She realizes that there are many special people in her life. Ron is one of those very special people, who over the years, continues to be willing to reach out to her. She hopes to always stay connected to Ron.

There's a beautiful country western song titled, **_Holes in the Floor of Heaven_**. The song says that raindrops are the tears of joy of our loved ones that have died. Tears of the heart have a special healing power too. Just ask Lesa.

SHARKS AND HEROES MADE OF STEEL

By

Charles McKee

The town of Fredericksburg, Texas is about sixty miles northwest of San Antonio off Highway 10. It is a small community with a strong German culture. This quaint and patriot Texas town is the home of the Admiral Nimitz Museum and state historical park.

I was first introduced to Fredericksburg during my coverage of "Up Periscope" for Military magazine, and its publisher, my old friend and Viet Nam war correspondent, Armond Noble.

Over three days, I met many of our country's most heroic and respected Americans. This assignment was an examination and review of Submarine Operations in the Pacific theater of World War II from 1941-1945.

My service was also in the United States Navy, but always on surface ships. My ship, USS Jarvis DD799, a destroyer, sailed in many of the waters where the Pacific campaigns were fought. I often wondered what it must have been like to serve in submarines during combat operations.

My historical finding found that seven separate U.S. submarine commanders received the "Medal of Honor", our nation's highest award for valor during combat.

These men are of course the indomitable, Rear Admiral (then Commander) Richard H. O'Kane, then aboard USS Tang SS 306 ; Rear Admiral Eugene B. Fluckey (then Commander) aboard USS Barb SS 220; Vice Admiral L.P. "Red" Ramage , (then Commander) aboard USS Parche SS 384; and Captain,(then Commander) George Street III aboard USS Tirante SS 420.

While the magazine coverage spotlighted the only four living World War II Submarine Commanders to receive the " Medal of Honor"; it must be remembered that three other men were also awarded with the medal for their extreme heroism while in command, and during war time operations.

They were: Samuel D. Dealy, (Commander) USS Harder SS 257; John P. Cromwell, (Captain) USS Skulpin SS 191; and Howard W. Gilmore, (Commander) USS Growler SS 215. These gallant submarine commanders gave their lives for their crews and for the United States of America; and in doing so, received the" Medal of Honor" posthumously.

The heroic actions of these "Submarine Skippers" are the foundations for many of the famous Submarine movies regarding the second world was that wrote into history the heroic crews and their famous boats. Sadly, as is the case with all of our World War Two veterans, all of the remaining four Sub-Commanders have left for their eternal patrols.

"All ships can submerge, but only Submarines can resurface." Chester W. Nimitz, 3-20-89, Fredericksburg, Texas.

THOSE DARING YOUNG MEN

By

Ron Corbin

During the Vietnam War, there was a special group of young men who were placed in Uncle Sam's combat military aircraft to fight what would become known as "The Helicopter War." Some of these young aviators were as young as nineteen when they became aircraft commanders of million dollar flying machines.

When President Johnson started the build-up of American troops being sent to Southeast Asia in the mid-1960s, the Army quickly realized that there was going to be a need for a large number of pilots to fly helicopters, especially the Bell UH-1 Iroquois commonly known as the "Huey." In order to fill this need, the Army decided to take a chance on eighteen-year-olds with only a high school diploma. To others, it looked like the Army needed an expendable source of manpower.

The other military branches, Navy, Marines and Air Force, were requiring their pilot candidates to be college graduates, which meant that they were closer to the age of twenty-two before they could even start pilot training. Even after these military services lowered their standards to that of a two-year college education in order to fill their quotas for the Vietnam effort, it still meant that after their aviator training programs, a Navy/Marine or Air Force pilot would be close to their mid-twenties before piloting an aircraft.

Four years difference in maturity was going to be a risk for the Army by allowing someone to command their combat aircraft. Yet these were young men who could offer their lives in service to their country, had barely started to shave. They were also determined by law not responsible enough to even drink alcoholic beverages. These potential Army pilots were even under society's legal age of twenty-one for making a decision to get married without their parents' signature. It was a gamble that the Army was willing to risk, but one that later would prove to have paid-high dividends in mission accomplishment and tremendous success.

When the Army began their WORWAC (Warrant Officer Rotary Wing Aviation Course) flight program for high school graduates in the 1960s, their goal was to train as many pilots as they could. The chance of becoming an Army helicopter pilot and going to Vietnam was almost a "given." A nine month program, five at Fort Wolters in north central Texas and four at Ft. Rucker in southern Alabama, approximately 250 pilots were graduating each month. By 1967, that had more than doubled.

The tremendous need for Army helicopter pilots came for two primary reasons. First, the success of the helicopter's versatility was being evidenced on a daily basis for combat support to ground troops; in troop movement, resupply, medevac, and armed gunship support. During the Vietnam War, almost nine million flight hours were logged in Army helicopters, with nearly eighty-eight percent being in Hueys. Records also show that out of 7,013 Hueys serving in the Vietnam War, there were 3,305 destroyed. Almost all were Army.

Secondly, there were a lot of casualties among helicopter crews. Out of 37,500 Army helicopter pilots, 1,869 were killed. The majority of these, two-thirds, were in the warrant officer ranks. The youngest to be killed was WO1 Raymond H. Chase, Jr., KIA 10 Nov 1967. He was just 19.3 years-old. The average tour length for a helicopter pilot before being killed was just 154 days; less than half of their assigned deployment period.

So what was the attraction for thousands of young men, with many having just graduated from high school, to gravitate towards a profession of flying a machine that even just the aerodynamics of which has been questioned by so many? What made them desire to be placed in harm's way that they surely knew they would encounter with the Vietnam War?

As one of those young Army warrant officers, I personally know it wasn't for the money. In fact, the love of flying made it difficult for me to understand that I was getting paid for something that I truly loved doing.

I strongly believe these young men had the same allure that has drawn men to flying since the Wright brothers. In flying, there is something adventurous about defying Newton's Law of Gravity.

There is something about the adventure of aerial freedom. There is something about the dauntless challenge of having so much power and control over something that few others can claim. There is something about "living on the edge" of life when you are young and have first achieved a sense of personal freedom from cutting the strings of your mother's apron. And maybe even to some degree, there is something about the perception of charm that a flight suit has for the opposite sex.

Ask any troop who set foot on the jungle floors of South Vietnam what their most vivid sound memory was from their time spent in combat. I can almost guarantee that most will say it was the "Whop-Whop-Whop" sound of a Huey's rotor blades. It was the Huey that meant more ammo, water, C-rations, and even mail from home were on the way. It was the Huey that called forth the fear of going into battle, as well as the relief of that fear when being removed from the battlefield. It was the Huey whose rockets and mini-guns suppressed enemy action. For some who were wounded or dying, it was the sound of those blades that became the beating wings of their "Angel of Mercy."

Behind the sounds of the Huey were young Army aviators who were still too young to realize that they were invincible. Day or night, these daring young men in their flying machines, put mission accomplishment first. Thousands became unsung heroes to their fellow aviators and comrades on the ground. But to each other they were just kids who had only months before traded-in their high school street rod for an aerial thrill of racing among the clouds. This would become the historical record for the Army's Warrant Officer Aviation Program.

VIVA LA TROOP

A Hero in Scouts Clothing

By

Charles McKee

Herb Holland: Boy Scout Troop Master, US Army Artillery Major, Korean War, and motivator of young boy scouts, hero and friend.

Any professional football team would hire Herb Holland to fill the position of linebacker as he was thick, strong, and more than able. His thick brown curly hair sat atop of a thick muscular neck by connected itself to a thick strong and round chest.

His steely blue eyes and smiling face may have fooled many folks, but, we scouts in troop 123, Richmond, California knew him for his strength of character and leadership qualities.

I met the scout master just a week before I officially joined Troop 123. His vise like grip welcomed me into the troop, and convinced my father that I would grow into a motivated and loyal scout.

My dad had served as a scout master in our home town of Raton, New Mexico. His troop frequented the famous Philmont Scout Ranch within easy driving distance of our hometown.

My family had an opportunity to be stationed at Philmont as Scouting Rangers assigned to work at the great ranch. The raging Second World War, and other family needs drove us instead to the industrial wartime city of Richmond, California.

Herb Holland wove unusual standards into troop 123. One of my fondest recollections was that our troop had its own song; often sung as fifty young scouts humped their military packs to distant camporee in a neighboring city easily reached by family cars. This troop often times began its marches as early as four am to allow time to arrive while we might best be seen by other competitive troops such as Troop 120 which also met at a nearby school.

Did I say that each new troop member had to be accepted by means of an initiation? I was twelve years of age; and had not experienced initiation into anything. I must assume my cohorts were equally excited as the moment of truth arrived.

I am sure that some nattering soul would surely try to stop Troop 123's initiation if it were suggested today. The precursor to the evening's festivities began with the caveat

"Do you trust your fellow scouts enough to undergo this initiation to become one of us?"

I can remember my father's words of encouragement as the initiation team began blindfolding each and every one of us. "Remember, everyone in this troop trusted their fellow scouts and they seemed to trust us enough to put us through the formal initiation." Join or leave were our choices. All seven of us joined that night; joined a troop that was led by a man among men.

In two hours time we believed we had stood at the rim of the Grand Canyon; ate worms for dinner; walked over a bridge that swayed and bucked in the evening breeze. When we were unable to produce an official boy scout canteen, we carried a quart of water in our pants pockets as two girls laughed out loud while calling our names.

There were so many honorable men and women in our young lives, they were truly patriots and heroes all.

"A friend on my left and a friend on my right

Viva La 123

A willing endeavor we all will unite

Viva La 123

Viva La, Viva La, Viva La Troop

Viva La, Viva La, Viva La Troop

Viva La Troop

Viva La Troop

Viva La 123."

WEEKEND WARRIORS

By

Jack Miller

From the first day in high school I knew I was going to be a US Army soldier.

I went to high school in Calumet Michigan. For those unfamiliar with the area, Calumet is in the Keweenaw Peninsula of Upper Michigan. Calumet High School had the first Junior Reserve Officer Training Corp (JROTC) in Michigan. Each of the four grades had about 150 students for a total of 600 high school students. Half of the students in Calumet High were male and of those a little more than half, about 175, of the male students were JROTC cadets. We had three retired army personnel assigned as instructors; a Major in charge, a Master Sergeant and a Sergeant First Class. All three were professional soldiers who had been in service during WWII.

In 1949, as a fourteen year old, I was rather small compared to the athletic types, so naturally I opted to take JROTC. We were issued olive drab colored uniforms just like real soldiers. We marched and we had classes. We polished our brass and our shoes and ironed our uniforms because we did not want to anger any of our instructors. They taught us how to disassemble all of the small arms, and more importantly how to put them back together blindfolded, using all the parts. A feat not easily accomplished even by some professional soldiers. They taught us the history of the armed forces of the United States of America. We learned military traditions and tactics. What I enjoyed most was being on the rifle team and learning how to shoot correctly and safely, learning to do it the army way.

After four years, I felt I knew everything about the army. I was eager to go to college, get a degree and receive a commission. I set my sights on the Michigan College of Mining and Technology; they too had a ROTC program.

When everything seems to be going right, you have obviously overlooked something. I did. My father had to go into a sanitarium for Tuberculosis and I became the head of the house and the bread winner. I worked at the one industry in town, the Calumet and Hecla Consolidated Copper Company. Things were okay for a while; my dream had been shattered but stuff happens. What mattered was that I was contributing to the support of our family. Then the price of copper fell and they began laying people off. I was one of the first to go. I drew unemployment for about two months then I enlisted in the Army. Part of my dream would come to fruition even if I was only an enlisted soldier.

On January 31, 1955, I went to Milwaukee, Wisconsin for the physical and induction. The other enlistees and I walked around in our underwear being poked and prodded and the Army concluded that I was fit for duty. A group of about thirty of us were placed in a room and we began waiting. Time dragged on, and it got later and later. Finally, an officer came in and announced that the Army had met its quota. They could not accept any more volunteers for the month of January. They did take all the draftees. He then announced we could wait around until after midnight when it would be February, get sworn in and leave for basic training. Then he dropped another bomb on us. If we did wait until after midnight we would not be eligible to receive any rights under the GI Bill of rights. Education benefits and mustering out pay were the two most important rights we would not get. About half the men got up and left. The rest of us stayed. We ate a box lunch provided by the army, and sat around talking until just after midnight. Then we were called to attention, sworn in, loaded on a bus and driven to Fort Leonard Wood, Missouri, where our eight weeks of basic training began. After that, it was on to Camp Gordon, Georgia for Military Police (MP) training, which was what I requested when I enlisted.

Things were going right for a change. After another eight weeks of MP training, we were informed that our assignments were posted on the Company bulletin board. I almost cried when I saw I was going to be a prison guard. In my mind I was the most knowledgeable soldier in the company, fully trained to perform police duty, and I would be guarding military prisoners. Not only that, it would be of all places, right there at Camp Gordon, soon to be renamed Fort

Gordon. My heart sank as the other, lesser soldiers received their assignments to cities in the US and overseas to perform real military police duty. None the less, orders are orders.

I worked in the guard towers and I rode shotgun over military prisoners who had violated the law and had been found guilty of their crimes by courts martial. Every one of the 1200 prisoners we supervised had been tried, convicted, found guilty and had been sentenced to at least one year at hard labor. They would also receive a Bad Conduct or Dishonorable discharge. After eight months, I was promoted to Private First Class and with that, a change of duty. Now I would be thrust among the prisoners, working inside the wire, within a locked compound containing 300 prisoners. My coworkers would be two other PFC's and a sergeant; we would be badly outnumbered.

Prisoners are a funny lot, at least ours were. Almost all of them would have put back on the uniform and fought for our country if it were necessary. They had disgraced the uniform but they were still patriotic. Unfortunately for them, but fortunate for the United States, there was no military emergency… not yet.

Often if you pray hard enough for something, God answers. I did not like being a prison guard; I wanted Military Police duty. I developed a skin disease, which I believe God sent me, and the Army did the rest. I was sent to the dermatology clinic for treatment and I was hospitalized. Even though the doctor who ran that clinic saw more patients in a day than the rest of the hospital did collectively, She only had one medic, one receptionist and three ward supervisors assigned to her. She supplemented her staff with patients who were willing to work. My skin disease was cured within ten days, but she asked me if I wanted to remain as a patient for six more months while working for her. I jumped at the opportunity, especially when she told me that after six months I would be transferred from Fort Gordon to someplace near my home.

Three other patients and I swept and scrubbed floors, cleaned toilets, straightened chairs and magazines. One patient was trained to perform EKG's while another patient scheduled appointments, and another ran errands. I was given the honor of working with her medic and wore a white jacket while giving simple treatments. The patients I helped never knew I was not a medic and I was closely watched by the medic. After six months, I received orders transferring me from Fort Gordon to Fort Wayne, Detroit, Michigan. I would no longer be a prison guard; I would don a white hat, a sidearm and a nightstick and be a Military Policeman.

Fort Wayne was an army reserve center. Reservists would come to Fort Wayne to perform their required two weeks annual active duty. We active duty personnel disparagingly referred to them as "weekend warriors" not real soldiers like us. We were the ones who had volunteered to protect our nation, the week end warriors were really draft dodgers in disguise. That is how most of us regular army soldiers felt, that the reservists were lesser soldiers.

One evening I was dressed my sharpest and assigned as the main gate guard. I was really a glorified information post but I was regular army. It was early evening when a taxicab pulled up and a man got out. He was dressed in civilian clothes. He pulled out a suit case and his large duffle bag and tossed them to the sidewalk. He paid the cabbie who turned around and left.

Here is another weekend warrior I thought.

I was right. He showed me his orders and asked where he had to go to sign in. I gave him the instructions to the Headquarters building; up one block, turn right and walk another block. In reading his orders I noted he was a captain and I thought, *good, the exercise won't hurt him. It will get him in shape for his two weeks active duty.*

He asked if we had a post taxi and I told him no, we didn't. I could have called the desk and had the patrol unit swing by and give him a lift, but I didn't. After all he was only a week-end warrior. He asked if he could leave his bags there in the gate shack while he went to sign in. Again, I told him he could not, as we could not be responsible for his property, even though we had done it for others. Off he went carrying his suitcase and his duffle bag. I didn't even salute him. *(I snickered to myself, because I put that week-end warrior in his place. I showed him who the true patriots and heroes were. It was us regulars, not week-end warriors.)*

I had the same post the next night. It was just after dark when the same captain-weekend warrior came walking towards the gate house. This time he was in uniform and this time I saluted. We talked for about thirty seconds about Fort Wayne and the Detroit area. I noticed he had several rows of colorful ribbons and the Combat Infantryman's Badge, that blue bar with the rifle in the center awarded to soldiers who had been in actual combat and I began to feel quite small. But my shame came when I saw the solid light blue ribbon with the small white stars on it. The Captain was not only a combat veteran, he had been awarded the Medal of Honor, the highest military award any soldier can receive and is awarded as a result of bravery.

It was then I realized that there was more to the army than I knew. He was a patriot, a hero and a week end warrior. Suddenly, for me I learned the difference. Some of us can be heroes. All of us can be patriots.

From that time on, no National Guardsman, no reservist, either officer or enlisted, ever had to walk from my post to headquarters to sign in. It was also the last time I ever referred to them as Week End Warriors. They were and are warriors in every sense of the word.

FRENCH DAVIS

By

Robert M. Cawley

I use to get tired of people asking me if I *really* knew French Davis. Yeah, I know French. In fact, I knew French when he had both arms and both eyes. French and I were at Greenbrier Military School [prep school & junior college] in the fall of 1941. You remember 1941 when the Japanese attacked Pearl Harbor and set off World War II.

French was a good looking college freshman. He was the commander of the band, a member of the honor court, the rifle team, the varsity wrestling team, varsity track team, and played a great jazz trumpet, plus he was one of the best drum majors the school ever had. He was looking forward to one more year at Greenbrier then off to a four year college to start pre-med. I was trying to figure out how to survive the academic life and was not certain I would be around for future years. As it turned out destiny was about to change both our worlds.

On Sunday, December 7, 1941, when Pearl Harbor was attacked Colonel J.M. Moore let every single member of the 500 plus cadet corps make a five minute call home. I guess like most of the guys I told my dad I wanted to leave school and join the Marine Corps. His answer was: "Stay in school, there's going to be war enough for everyone." Of course he was right but the next morning at mess formation we all had nothing but envy when Fred Andrews from California was picked up and taken to the train station to join the armed forces. His father had said he could go. Six months later Fred was the first of our school to die in combat when he was killed in a naval engagement in the Pacific.

A couple of days later the school was notified that all cadet officers who were college freshmen or above would report to Ft. Thomas, Kentucky, when school was out where they would be commissioned as 2nd Lieutenants in the Army. French would be among them.

At Fort Thomas French gave basic training to raw recruits, most of them older men in the citizen army. He requested transfer to the Army Air Corps to take pilot training. The request was pigeon-holed. Then he applied for airborne, but before any action could be taken on that application he was transferred to a cavalry unit at Camp Adair, Oregon. Within a few days of reporting to Camp Adair, he received a summons to report to the CO at regimental headquarters. On doing so he was ushered into the office of a colonel who proceeded to ask him how the mother of the Greenbrier president and all the Moore family were doing. Needless to say, French had many unanswered questions rolling around his brain until the colonel informed him that he had been one of the government inspection team who had judged the Best Drilled Platoon in

1941, and remembered that French was the platoon commander. He advised French that he was happy to have him aboard and cut orders to be processed to promote him to first lieutenant. Before those orders came through our young officer was transferred to the 506 regiment of the 101st Airborne Division at Camp Toccoa, Georgia. The cavalry unit in Oregon never left the United States.

Our young first lieutenant then was sent to Ft. Benning, Georgia, where he met a beautiful young lady named Bettye Roberts and they were married. The next stop was the war in Europe.

At an airstrip outside of Rome, French was going over basic instructions with his men prior to combat when a defective pin in the hand grenade he was holding fell out and the grenade was activated. In a split second he had to make a decision. Throw the grenade as far as possible and kill and wound some of his men… or, he yelled for them to scatter then fell on the grenade taking the full impact of the explosion.

When he awoke in a field hospital he realized that he had lost both arms below the elbow as well as his left eye. This certainly altered any future plans he might have had, but the biggest worry was how this would affect his marriage. Back home Bettye had taken her marriage vows very seriously and remained at his side through good times and bad for fifty-seven years when she passed away.

After a long hospitalization he returned to his hometown of Clendennin, West Virginia, and was unable to find a job for a returned veteran who had hooks instead of hands. He opened a taxi business then graduated to the used car business with his brother. In the meantime, he became a speed typist with his hooks. The brother wanted to attend medical school so the business was sold and French, with wife Bettye and two young daughters in tow they made the move to Daytona Beach, Florida.

Put yourself in this young man's place. Yes, he had the devotion of his wife and family, but what had happened to the promise of a fine, productive life? Although I don't think he ever perceived himself as handicap, the rest of the world did and somehow he had to create a world for himself and his loved ones.

He could have recalled the lines by Horace Greely. "Fame is but a vapor, popularity an accident; Riches take wing. Those who cheer you today will curse you tomorrow. One thing endures; character." Character he had in abundance. It had been shaped and molded in the class rooms, on the drill field and in athletic competition at Greenbrier and in the darkest hours that Character prevailed.

He graduated with a Law degree from John Stetson University in 1952 and opened his office in Daytona Beach. This was rather difficult since he had a wife, two small daughters, and no money. The Veterans Administration let arm amputees purchase a $1,500 car and they would pay for it.

Since he already had a car he made a deal with the Kaiser-Frazer Agency to process paperwork on a car that would stay on their lot. When the Agency got the check they deducted $50.00 for their trouble and the balance was used to open his law office where he did his own typing and answered his own phones.

And so the things that would have proved too much to conquer for other men no longer affected his goals. He still enjoys the practice of law and for fifteen years was a judge. In one well known action he appealed a case from the County Court to the Circuit Court, then to the Court of Appeals and eventually wound up in the Florida Supreme Court. This process took over five years to complete, but he was finally successful and the Supreme Court ruled with him. This case changed the procedure of all law enforcement officers in the State of Florida, including all city police, sheriff's officers and the Florida Highway Patrol.

He has also taken cases before the prestigious House Judiciary Committee.

I asked French what Greenbrier gave him that became a part of his life when school days were over. This is what he told me. "Greenbrier provided inspiration and a challenge to everyone that the good things you want are there and you too can have them provided you put forth the effort. This philosophy is something you didn't leave at school but something you took with you and something you have realized to be true every day of your life. The school instilled a sense of loyalty and did import the adage that if a thing is worth doing it is worth doing well and it certainly taught tenacity – stay with the job until it is finished." French Davis... *A very special man.*

ANGELS ALSO GET BRONZE STARS

By

Charles McKee

The Vietnam War continued to rage in Southeast Asia. Rumors were spreading that we would be leaving the Republic of Vietnam, in the not too distant future.

Returning combat veterans could be found in any part of San Francisco, Oakland and North Bay area communities. I doubt seriously that many vets would identify themselves as residents of Berkeley; although it was within the bay area.

Berkeley had brought much heartburn for the military and the surrounding bay area law enforcement agencies. Most of the anti-war and anti-USA protests began in Berkeley; although San Francisco street demonstrations began with the Auto Row violence on Van Ness Avenue.

Most police calls for assistance were rooted in massive demonstrations on the University of California (UC) Berkeley, or San Francisco State College campuses. My first assignment was as a member of the second platoon of Oakland Police Officers to arrive in support of then UC president Clark Kerr, and the overpowered UC Berkeley Police Department. It was referred to as the Sproul Hall demonstrations, and found its way into American history.

I changed law enforcement agencies in the late 1960s, and joined the Contra Costa County Sheriff's Department, the bordering county to the North of Alameda County where UC Berkeley is located.

The last months of 1968 brought trouble to all of the North Bay area cities as they responded to the requests for law enforcement assistance between San Francisco, Oakland and Berkeley. The pattern of twelve hour shifts lasted through 1970 giving all Bay area law enforcement officers the opportunity to deal with massive street demonstrations highlighted with numerous arrests and ample opportunities for the use of tear gas.

I was surely getting tired of the overtime, as well as attending a college that required a round trip drive of 140 miles three times a week.

My eventual transfer to a specialized anticrime unit brought me into contact with many circumstances that reminded me of my service in the busy city of Oakland.

Police Officers are often called upon to visit hospitals several times a week as injured victims are delivered to them for life saving care. Pittsburg Emergency Hospital was one of our routine assignments as they provided critical care for all of the county unincorporated area surrounding the relatively small city of Pittsburg, California.

On one such visit, I found it necessary to contact one of the nurses working the emergency room on a busy Friday evening. My first opinion of her was less than flattering, as law enforcement officers have a good working relationship with most medical and emergency services providers.

This hardcore little blond nurse was the exception to the rule. She was not one to joke with, and to try to get her to stop for information was next to impossible.

I had just about written her off as a "jerk nurse" who was somewhat filled with herself, and her position as emergency room nurse.

I relayed my thoughts to a young male doctor one evening following a shooting in nearby Columbia Park area. Needless to say I received an ear full.

It seems this spunky nurse was a recently discharged army combat nurse just having returned from Vietnam. Not only did this hardcore lady do a tour there, she was right in the middle of heavy combat.

It seemed the young male doctor was also a recently returned veteran who knew the story of her combat exploits.

One evening nurse this brave nurse was in the emergency operating room of the military hospital at Tuy Hua, Vietnam. She had been assisting with an unusually high number of wounded troops. The North Vietnam Army (NVA) decided that, hospital or not, it was time to send a rather long barrage of mortar shells upon the hospital.

The hospital position was made worse when word came that the Communist NVA intended to take the camp at all costs.

Well, the NVA tried, and they rocketed the hospital without rest for some days. Nearby army units recommended they abandon the hospital and move the troops out of the coming maelstrom. The doctors and nurses refused, and remained tending to the wounded during the mortar barrage.

Our hero nurse would receive the Army's bronze star with a "V" device. That device signifies valor in the face of the enemy.

Some weeks later I stopped her on a less than busy evening and shook her hand and thanked her for such tremendous courage and commitment to our troops.

And, in her style as hero, nurse and American, she said: "What? I didn't do anything."

But, then that's what all heroes say.

THE ATROCITY OF WAR

By

Robert Fregeau

I recently completed reading two non-fictional tomes relating to World War Two; *Flags of Our Fathers* by James Bradley and *Unbroken* by Laura Hillenbrand. I have never been held spellbound by anything in my life as these two tomes. The overriding facts I took away from these readings were; man's inhumanity to man and the resilience of the human mind and body to overcome the horrors from the acts of war.

While this is not a review of the works themselves, they stand as a platform for the research contained in this document. Without going into ancient history, I cite World War One as the beginning war in modern history for the use of tactical atrocities. It began on April 15, 1915 at the battle for Ypres, Belgium with the use of chlorine gas by the German army against the English, French and Canadian soldiers. In the coming months, use of chemical toxins escalated to the use of Phosgene and Mustard gases. While the gas causality rate is unknown, its use did not discriminate between civilian and military populations. A little known by-product from the use of chemicals in World War I was that Adolf Hitler was a victim of its use. In World War II he refused the use of battlefield gasses but chose their use in his extermination camps.

World War II brought about the most egregious and horrendous acts of pain and suffering known to modern man. In the pacific theater of operations, it was the American servicemen and women along with their English and Australian counterparts who suffered the most dehumanizing treatment at the hands of the Japanese Army and Navy.

For Americans, it was the prisoner of war (POW) who suffered most at the hands of the Japanese. Their crimes were not limited to forced labor, but resulted in mass execution of American civilian workers; e.g. Wake Island, 98 POW's. The Bataan Death March was the foundation for the starvation, bayoneting and beheading of as many as 10,600 American and Filipino prisoners.

Captured Americans also became subjects of medical experiments both in Japan and in occupied China. Vivisection was often used without the use of anesthesia. Perhaps the most egregious act took place on Iwo Jima where a Mount Suribachi flag-raising marine found his friend disemboweled and his severed genitals in his mouth.

And in the modern-day era of warfare they call "water boarding" torture?

AUDIE MURPHY

By

Robert M. Cawley

He was born to a poverty stricken family of cotton sharecroppers on June 20, 1924. He rose to fame in World War II as America's most decorated hero. He was the recipients of 24 decorations including the Congressional Medal of Honor before his 21st birthday. All America knew who he was when his photo appeared on the cover of Life Magazine on June 10, 1945. Soon the entire world was aware of AUDIE MURPHY. At that point in time he planned to become a career army man but destiny had other ideas.

Motion picture icon James Cagney saw the Life photo. Cagney realized in Audie with his soft Texas voice, good looking youthful looks, plus the fact that he was America's most decorated soldier as a sure bet for motion picture stardom. Cagney signed him to a contract to make films for his company. Like it does so many times, best laid plans fail. Audie came to California and lived at Cagney's home for over a year. When nothing worked out Audie moved out and started looking for movie work. His first break came in 1947. A small part in "Beyond Glory" a Paramount film that starred Alan Ladd with Donna Reed. The screenplay saw Ladd and Murphy as West Point cadets. The critics liked Audie and a long career was born.

Slowly he picked up better acting assignments but a big lift to his career came in 1949 when his autobiography "To Hell And Back" was published sending him on a tour of the Southwest book signings. Later the book became a best seller and critics praised it as "a masterpiece." Rejected by both the marines and airborne because he was too small Audie was determined to serve his country. Serve it he did in the army infantry in battles in Sicily, Italy, France and Germany. He was credited with having killed, captured or wounded 240 Germans in a single engagement.

Audie's acting in the classic "The Red Badge Of Courage" should have earned him an Academy Award for his portrayal of a coward who ran in the face of battle. The MGM release fell short due to the fact that director John Huston did not edit the film but left it in the studio's hands which is always a tragic mistake. Huston rushed off to Africa to direct Bogart and Hepburn in "The African Queen" robbing Audie of the award critics felt he deserved.

Like millions of others I followed Murphy's military and cinema careers with great interest and always wondered what the man behind the legend was like. I got my answer in 1952 when a publicity person from Universal-International called me and asked if I would be interested having Audie as a guest on my hour long, six day a week television show on KPHO-TV, Phoenix, Arizona. He was going to be in town for three days, with beautiful Susan Cabot to promote his new film, "The Duel At Silver Creek" which by the way included a bit player named Lee Marvin who was not a part of the tour.

This was an offer I couldn't refuse. I told the Universal people that I would give Audie and Susan the bulk of my one hour production and if it could fit into their schedule, would have them back on the third day for a spot review of the film, a western.

Audie had married Pamela Archer in April of 1951 following his divorce from actress Wanda Hendrix. Pamela and Audie were expecting their first child in March. Soon to arrive in Phoenix. Soldier, actor, soon to be father and citizen.

When we first met he reminded me of a cat who had lived with a great deal of trauma in his life and you take him into your home. Like a cat he was very wary of strangers until he got to know you. The thing that brought us together fast was our mutual love of music. 1 had no idea he was a song writer but over the years his songs were recorded by name artists like Jimmy Dean, Dean Martin, Charlie Pride, Roy Clark, Eddy Arnold, Jerry Wallace, Teresa Brewer, and Porter Waggoner. Audie was very impressed by a singer/guitarist I had hired to do a twelve minute segment of my show. Marty Robbins, who would become a country music icon, was singing a song I had written titled "Raindrops On My Window And Teardrops In My Heart." In 1962 Audie and co-writer Scott Turner wrote "Shutters and Boards." Recorded by Jerry Wallace, it sold over 600,000 copies.

I was surprised to find that Audie was also a poet and should have been published. He started writing during the war and his work was the equal of any first class writer. You have to remember he was forced to quit school after the fifth grade to go to work as a farm hand. This makes his many achievements all the more remarkable.

On camera we talked about his film and Susan Cabot added a lot of beauty to the set. Off camera we never spoke of war with the exception that Audie wanted Universal to finance a film based on his life and book, "To Hell And Back." That did come true in 1955. A big budget film it proved a huge success. What we did talk about was the baby that was on its way and how much he wanted a family. He was very aware that having a family meant having a steady income and although hoping for better roles in better stories he signed a long term contract with Universal. He joked that he would "probably make thirty or forty westerns for the studio because they made money but the only change in the films would be the horses." He was very prophetic. He made 33 westerns during his career.

The Universal publicist had brought along starlet Yvette Dugay and up and coming young actors Jim Best and John Hudson to introduce to the press and radio stations. They all made a brief appearance on my show but were being hustled from place to place by the publicist which gave Audie and me more time together.

He loved kids, the outdoors and animals. He was a very nice person to know, and very interesting. Citizen Murphy could have been the guy next door. Before he left Phoenix we promised to keep tabs on each other via the mail.

That always sounds good but the truth was that after a couple of months the notes dropped off and then vanished. The only two celebrities who didn't drop off my radar were composer Johnny Mercer who wrote fabulous memo pad notes and pianist, composer, band leader Frankie Carle who would write long letters.

The Murphy's first child was a boy they named Terry and two years later son James arrived.

Audie enjoyed a steady career and once in awhile got a role that let him expand his range as an actor. Fans and critics alike loved him in "To Hell And Back." However they wanted him in westerns and were happy when he co-starred with Jimmy Stewart in "Night Passage" although Audie played the role of an outlaw. In 1960 Audie gave what should have been an award winning performance by a supporting actor in "The Unforgiven," a western, that starred Burt Lancaster and Audrey Hepburn and was directed by John Huston.

I would have liked to have known Audie Murphy better. Not because of his military record or his work in films, but as a friend. A regular guy who had a great love of life. He could hold an intelligent conversation on many subjects and was fun to be with.

Audie died May 28, 1971 along with five business partners in the crash of their private plane during a rainstorm twenty miles south of Roanoke, Virginia. He was buried at Arlington National Cemetery with full military honors.

His wife Pamela worked at the Veterans Administration Hospital in Los Angeles until her death in the early 2000's.

AUDIE MURPHY MILITARY HONORS:

MEDAL OF HONOR

DISTINGUISHED SERVICE CROSS

SILVER STAR WITH OAK LEAF CLUSTER

LEGION OF MERIT

BRONZE STAR AND FIRST OAK LEAF CLUSTER

CROIX DE GIERRE WITH PALM [FRANCE]

PURPLE HEART WITH OAK LEAF CLUSTERS

LEGION OF MERIT

BELGIAN CROIX DE GIERRE WITH PALM MEDAL OF LIBERATED FRANCE

FRENCH LEGION OF HONOR, GRADE OF CHEVALIER

GOOD CONDUCT MEDAL

AMERICAN CAMPAIGN MEDAL

EUROPEAN AFRICAN AND MIDDLE EASTERN CAMPAIGN MEDAL WITH ONE SILVER STAR, FOUR BRONZE SERVICE STARS (REPRESENTS 9 CAMPAIGNS, ONE BRONZE ARROWHEAD REPRESENTS ASSAULT LANDINGS AT SICILY AND SOUTHERN FRANCE]

DISTINGUISHERD UNIT EMBLEM WITH OAK LEAF CLUSTER

WORLD WAR II VICTORY MEDAL

ARMY OF OCCUPATION MEDAL WITH GERMANY CLASP

COMBAT INFANTRYMAN BADGE

MARKSMAN BADGE WITH RIFLE BAR

EXPERT BADGE WITH BAYONET BAR

VICTORY MEDAL

Lieutenant Audie Murphy was America's most decorated hero in World War II.

POLICE OFFICER EDDIE BYRNE MEMORIAL

By

Keith Bettinger

Saturday, October 14, 1989, was one of those beautiful autumn days when you want to take your kids to a football field to see an exciting game. It was not the type of day you want to see the field dedicated to the memory of a young man who played on that field not too many years before and because he was a police officer, was murdered in cold blood by drug dealers. But, there we were, law enforcement officers on the football field of Plainedge High School in North Massapequa, N. Y. as the field was dedicated to the memory of Police Officer Edward Byrne, murdered in 1988. The plaques donated by the New York State Fraternal Order of Police commemorating the field were mounted there on two brick columns, provided by the community.

I've attended quite a few police survival seminars, and I have worked as a counselor in Washington, D.C., for the Concerns of Police Survivors. During these experiences, I've learned that there is no fair trade-off when it comes to a cop's life being lost. No matter how many criminals fall, if we lose a cop, the price is too high. This is not to say that the "supreme sacrifice" was a waste, but, that it is too large a loss for the family, the department, and society to pay.

When Eddie was murdered, I never expected to see what followed. It all started with Mr. Byrne speaking to the media, asking the world to join the Byrne family at the funeral and deliver a message to the criminal element that we, as a society, would no longer tolerate their wanton behavior. I was amazed as I stood in formation and saw the people in attendance. I saw civilians, law enforcement officers, volunteer firemen with raised aerial ladders and an American Flag flying between them. I saw retired cops dressed in suits and ties, with mourning bands around their badges. They had retired from the force, but, not from the brotherhood. Eddie was speaking to the world louder than he ever could have on the streets where he worked. He was uniting society against a common enemy, and this was only the beginning.

On May 15, 1989, in Washington, D.C., at the National Law Enforcement Memorial Service, I heard President Bush speak of Eddie and his family. He said he is reminded of Eddie every day when he opens his desk drawer and sees Eddie's badge, which was given to him by Eddie's father. This tribute to Eddie was part of the President's "War on Drugs". Eddie may have been a casualty in this war, but, he is also one of its leaders.

In June 1989, at a Nassau County Police Conference meeting, I heard Mr. Byrne speak of Eddie and a drug program he and the Byrne family had established in Eddie's memory. This was the first I had heard of "Eddie's Kids". At this point, I came to understand how mourning can be channeled to a positive cause, and how Eddie was leading his family's war on drugs.

When I started my police career twenty years ago, schools and cops did not fare well together. Then, it seemed that it was cop verses the rest of the world. Who could have thought that twenty years later it would be cops, students, faculty, politicians and parents joined together on a football field with a twenty-two-year old cop, Eddie Byrne, as the common denominator? Who could possibly have ever thought that this young street cop could bring such a group together? But Eddie did.

I could have done without the speeches of the politicians. I didn't feel it was their day. I felt the day belonged to the Byrne family and the students and faculty of Plainedge High School. I was surprised when the principal introduced a distinguished alumnus, Steve Guttenberg, and announced him as the movie star of **Police Academy** and **Short Circuit** fame. Okay maybe I am a little dense, and didn't recognize him or his name at first. But do you know what? Eddie has probably become the most well known graduate of Plainedge High School.

Never did I expect to see cops and students united in a common endeavor, but there we stood — together, at Plainedge. On the field was a banner proudly announcing the students as "Eddie's Kids". The banner was signed by the students of Plainedge High School. This was a pledge to

Eddie and the world that they will not use drugs. No other twenty-two-year old street cop has ever accomplished such a goal.

The band performed a tribute and the choral groups sang. The girls' chorus sang Eddie's favorite song. His choice of music shows what a kind hearted, sensitive, twenty-two-year old the world lost. Eddie's favorite song was, **Somewhere Out There**, from the movie **An American Tail**. The song was beautiful, and brought tears to many eyes that day. When I listened to the lyrics, it gave me a whole new perspective on Eddie. His death is still a tragedy, but, in his short life he has accomplished more than any of us could ever hope to. It seems, when you listen to the music and the lyrics, it was composed just for Eddie.

**"Somewhere out there,
Beneath the pale moonlight,
Someone's thinking of me, and
Loving me tonight."**

Eddie, you'll never be forgotten. Your family and friends will always love you. They speak so lovingly when they mention your name. In every cop's heart, there's a space reserved for you, Eddie Byrne.

**"Somewhere out there,
Someone's saying a prayer-
That we'll find one another,**

In that big somewhere out there."

     Every night there are parents praying that their children grow up to be one of "Eddie's Kids". Children Eddie would be proud to know. Don't worry Eddie, maybe not in the near future, but someday during the span of infinity, there will be a long line of parents and cops waiting to shake your hand for all you've accomplished.

**"And even though I know how far apart we are,
It helps to think we might be wishing on the same bright star,
And when the night wind starts to sing a lonesome lullaby,
It helps to think we're sleeping underneath the same big sky."**

     You're not that far away, Eddie. I'm sure that bright star in the heavens is you looking over your "kids" and all the cops continuing your battle. I bet that night wind is you, telling everyone to continue on.

**"Somewhere out there,
If love can see us through,
We'll be together,
Somewhere out there,
Where dreams come true."**

     Eddie, the love of your family, friends, coworkers and your "kids" will see us through. We'll all be together fighting your fight, trying to make sure your dreams and wishes do come true.

EVERY FAMILY HAS A HERO OR A PATRIOT

By

Jack Miller

Every family has a hero or patriot. I think mine did, although I was hard pressed to select just one.

My family was kind of large. My grandmother and grandfather on my mother's side had seven kids, four girls and three boys. I don't know about my father's side except for one brother.

Dad always went by the name Jack Miller. He was adopted when he was thirty-three years old. His birth name was Harry Lynn Bondurant. He was a medic in World War One and became a Michigan State policeman all under the name of Jack Miller. I guess they did not do background investigations back in the 1920s.

My three aunts had a total of fourteen kids, mostly boys. In my family there were six kids, four girls, myself and another boy.

My three uncles were all in the military during the second war. One was a Seabee, one a Coast Guardsman and the other was in the navy. Two of the four bothers- in- law served, one in the army and one a Seabee. The other two brother-in laws were too young to be called. One brother-in-law, Jimmy Lyons, was wounded in Naples, Italy. All of them returned from the war alive. I guess we were quite lucky in that respect.

In my opinion my family's hero, and in this case, also a patriot, was my dad. Even though he had been in the first "Great War," he registered for the draft but was not called. In 1941 he was 42 years old, married with a family, and had an essential job. He expressed love for the United States in so many ways that I also feel he was a true patriot. I know he would have gladly served had he been called but his job, age and marital status came into play. He was a Michigan State Police Trooper when the war broke out. He was promoted to corporal and was appointed in charge of the State Police post at Marquette, Michigan in the Upper Peninsula (UP) because they had no available captains. They had all been drafted or were assigned to other posts.

Dad worked with the FBI identifying and capturing draft evaders, escapees from the POW camps and the Conscientious Objectors camp. There were a number of military posts and camps in the UP as well. He did get involved with some of the uniformed miscreants. With the essential iron ore mines, the copper mines, and the Soo Locks, as well as the other manufacturing plants producing military supplies, all of which were assumed to be a sabotage target, there was a definite need for police protection.

So in my mind my dad was an unsung hero as well as a patriot. If he were alive today, there is no doubt he, like many of the heroes of the time would probably say the same thing. I'm not a hero. I just did my job for the country I love.

Dad, that may be true. But in my eyes you are as much a hero and just as much a patriot as I hope to be.

However, there is one true decorated hero in my family. My nephew, Michael John Lyons of Scottsdale Arizona, the son of Jimmy Lyons

Distinguished Flying Cross Medal

Criteria:

Awarded to any officer or enlisted member of the United States armed forces who distinguishes himself or herself in combat in support of operations by "heroism or extraordinary achievement while participating in an aerial flight, subsequent to November 11, 1918." The decoration may also be given for an act performed prior to that date when the individual has been recommended for, but has not received the Medal of Honor, Distinguished Service Cross, Navy Cross, or Distinguished Service Medal. During wartime, members of the Armed Forces of friendly foreign nations serving with the United States are eligible for the award. It is also given to those who display heroism while working as instructors or students at flying schools.

CITATION TO ACCOMPANY THE DISTINGUISHED FLYING CROSS AWARD TO MICHAEL J. LYONS

"Airman First Class Michael J. Lyons distinguished himself by heroism while participating in aerial flight as a Combat Photographer aboard an HH-3E near Hue, Republic of Vietnam on 14 March 1968. On that date, Airman Lyons, in the face of hostile fire, participated in the attempted rescue of a downed pilot who was completely surrounded by hostile forces. After the helicopter was hit and driven off on a previous rescue attempt, Airman Lyons manned an M-60 machine gun and returned fire. Airman Lyons continued to fire on hostile positions after the helicopter was disabled and on fire until a safe landing area could be reached. The outstanding heroism and selfless devotion to duty displayed by Airman Lyons reflect great credit upon himself and the United States Air Force."

However, as always, there is the story behind the story and this is Mike's;

At the time, Mike was a combat motion picture cameraman with the Air Force serving in Detachment 7, 600th Photo Squadron, Da Nang Air Base, Vietnam. He had been assigned to a Jolly Green Giant rescue helicopter to capture on film the attempted rescue of a downed fighter pilot. The crew was composed of all volunteers. The film was intended to be released to the media to show the folks back home that we did all we could to save downed air crew members. The chopper crew was not very excited about having a photographer on board as they had to remove ammunition to compensate for the

160 pounds Mike weighed. Obviously, ammunition is one of the very important things you want to carry when you go into a hot combat zone. The ammo came off reluctantly and according to Mike the reluctance was evident but taken in stride. Later that day the helicopter was scrambled into action when an F-4 Phantom jet was downed in the Ashau Valley, just south of the DMZ.

They located the downed pilot, who marked his position on the ground by popping an orange smoke flare. As the helicopter moved into position to rescue the pilot they were met by a hail of bullets from enemy forces on the ground. The chopper pilot abandoned the first attempt and decided to approach from a different direction, one which might be safer for his crew and the pilot they were trying to rescue. Unfortunately, the second attempt was met with more withering ground fire from enemy forces and the helicopter began to burn while only a few hundred feet off the ground. The rescue attempt had to be aborted. The Para-Rescue crewman manned a M-60 machine gun in the doorway and returned fire.

The enemy ground fire became more intense. Mike decided that he would not be taken without a fight. He threw the $4,000 Arriflex camera he carried that day to the rear of the chopper and grabbed the other M-60 on the left side of the aircraft and fired at anything that moved. He had never been trained to fire an M-60 machine gun and learned later that it should have been fired in short bursts to avoid burning the gun up. Truth is, he held the triggers back until the last round fired and that precious ammo can was empty. With more than a little luck, and some divine intervention, the helicopter made it far enough away to land safely.

The Jolly Green crew lived to fight another day.

Mike, like other heroes, will say he was not a hero that day. He only did what he felt needed to be done. He felt he was going to be killed and was not going to go down easy. He, and many others say, the real heroes are the one who did not come back.

After being discharged from the Air Force, Mike first became a Phoenix Police officer, then a motivational speaker, and finally a very successful financial advisor. He will soon retire to spend time with a wife of forty-four years and his children and grandchildren.

One of the things he did when he returned from Vietnam was to place the medal and citation into his gun safe, hiding the event, lest some anti-war protestor see it. For more than twenty years his awards were buried in a dresser drawer. Finally, it became okay to be a Vietnam veteran in America. After his first visit to the Vietnam Memorial ("The Wall") he dusted off the medal and citation which now proudly hang in his office. Mike also made himself a promise…should anyone EVER take exception to his service in the United States Air Force, that person would be immediately invited to the nearest parking lot where he would kick his ass or die in the attempt.

Mike overcame his fears. He did what had to be done and he did it for others.

Good going Mike! You have made many people proud of your service and we thank you.

FAREWELL TO A FIREMAN

By

Keith Bettinger

What a tribute to a fireman who has answered his last alarm. My father, Lothar Bettinger, was a fifty-one year member of Westbury, New York Fire Department's Hose Company No. 1 and the Fire Police. He died two days before Thanksgiving in November 2008, and the Westbury Fire Department dealt with his death with dignity and grace. There was nothing we as a family could ask for that they didn't think of before hand and provide for us.

The funeral was delayed because my mother was in the hospital waiting to have a pacemaker implanted, and my family had to fly in from Las Vegas, NV. On Saturday afternoon, as we entered the funeral home for the first viewing, outside the front door was Engine 965, an engine from Hose Company No. 1 and next to the truck on the sidewalk, folded reverently, was my father's turnout gear. This was done both days during his funeral. It truly told the community someone special had died.

In between the daily services, we went to my sister and brother-in-law's home to rest and have dinner. Both nights of the funeral, Hose Company No.1 had food waiting for us. They relieved us of so much extra work and stress, and allowed my mother to rest between visiting sessions.

On Sunday night the department held its departmental services. Firefighters, both young and old took their turn standing honor guard at his casket and more than half the department attended the services in uniform. Many more attended in civilian attire. The department chaplain praised my father with a moving eulogy and each firefighter took the time to render a salute at his casket.

One Monday morning, as we left the funeral home for the journey to church for a funeral mass and the cemetery for internment, Westbury Fire Department was there once again. Engine 965 was his flower car and the pallbearers were his fellow firefighters. On the way to the church, we passed Westbury's main firehouse. As we approached, the flag was at half mast and the firehouse was decked in black and purple bunting. The siren sounded one last time for Dad. Firefighters stood at attention on the ramp and rendered a salute, and once again there was his neatly folded turnout gear signifying my father had answered his last alarm. The final moving tribute at the firehouse was an arch created by two tower ladders with one of the biggest American flags I have ever seen hanging between them for all of us to pass under. What an honor for a firefighter and a former sailor.

At the church, he was greeted by an honor guard and pall bearers of his fellow firefighters, who rendered salutes and carried him into church. At the end of the mass, he was treated with all the dignity and grace one could ask for from his friends.

Our family has a tradition of service to the village of Westbury. Besides my father's fifty-one years, my uncle has been a member of Westbury Fire Department for over sixty-five years. My brother-in-law has been a member for more than thirty years, and even I spent three years as a member many years ago. Even though we have a proud tradition in the volunteer fire service I was still moved by all that Hose Company No.1 and the entire Westbury Fire Department did for the Bettinger and Durnan families during this difficult time.

Thank you Westbury firefighters, your kindness and thoughtfulness will never be forgotten.

FAMILY TRAITS

By

Scott Decker

Tallness has always challenged Deckers. Johannes DeDecker. government administrator for New Amsterdam: descendant Isaac Decker of Staten Island—oyster boat captain on the Jersey side, plying the Fresh Kills: his son Richard Tyson Decker joining the Eleventh New Jersey Volunteers, guest of a Union hospital after Gettysburg: finally Bob Decker —my father—first born to the streets of Elizabeth, then a teenager finishing high school while farming alone in west Jersey, finally drafted for Korea. Each man standing five foot five - although frequently claiming five six.

War enveloped Europe—Nazis destroying mankind and our nation stood up. Uncle Johnny Decker joined the fight, leaving the city of Elizabeth, New Jersey, finding his place among the Eighth Air Force and the crew of The Wild Hare, a B-17 flying fortress carrying out missions across Holland, France, Poland and Germany, bombing factories, air bases, and refineries: flying during D-Day and in the Battle of the Bulge. Thirteen machine gun placements—the ball turret gun the smallest—defended The Hare. Nicknamed "Suicide Seat" the ball turret descended from the huge ship's belly, tiny in size for air drag reduction, requiring the smallest and toughest of the crew to man it—my Uncle, Sergeant John H. Decker.

Throughout 1943, after taking off from the safety of Suffolk England, six miles above the earth, Uncle John would rotate the plexi-glass sphere until twin machine guns pointed straight down and then squeeze inside. He placed his feet on steel rests—one for rotation, the second for radio control with the crew. He crouched into a fetal position and buckled the safety belt tight before turning two locking hatch bolts overhead. Air supplied by tubes from oxygen bottles, frost-bite a constant companion, he sat with back and head against the rear wall of his plastic bubble, hips at the bottom, legs in mid-air. His eyes level with the fifty-caliber barrels spanning the turret's width, nearing either side of his neck. Cocking the guns by pulling wire cables, reaching around ammo boxes stacked above, careful not to disturb belts of brass bullets lying at his elbows, he focused on the gun sight hanging from above and descending between his feet as he scanned the air for thin, light Messerschmitts and newer, heavier Focke-Wulfs.

November came and with its eleventh day, mission number thirty-three. This time, a substitute. Uncle Johnny would sit out for a needed rest, a newer gunner taking his seat. Over Munster, Germany, The Wild Hare released her eight bombs and turned for England as Major Schnoor, the rising Luftwaffe Ace, powered his Focke-Wulf upward. Flak hit The Hare's third engine, then three more strikes. She dropped from the protection of her squadron and into the path of Major Schnoor. Twenty-millimeter cannons punched holes through her aluminum skin as fires ignited explosions and parachutes opened above Nazis in Holland.

Uncle Johnny returned to Elizabeth in 1945, surviving thrice weekly missions over German-held Europe. As he aged, he often seemed lost in thought, silent and preoccupied, never able to stay warm—remembering the numbness of cramped and frozen joints as he crouched in the bubble, eight to ten hours a stretch, wind blowing through, ice clogging oxygen masks, temperatures reaching forty, even sixty below, metal for a seat—wondering at his luck escaping Major Schnoor's cannon-fire, unaware his feet pedaled silently back and forth as he spun the turret and radioed his crew.

JOSEPH MARION "IAN" MOORE

By

Robert M. Cawley

Three years ago, Don Vermeulen, who graduated from Greenbrier Military School as a Cadet Captain stood before a white cross, one of thousands on this peaceful field in France that bore the name of J.M. Moore, 2nd Lieutenant who had died in combat with Patton's Army. For Don, and for all of us who knew Lieutenant Moore it was a moment to remember. "Ian" as he as he was called by his family, had been our schoolmate and friend.

I have many memories of "Ian" and his kindness and friendship to me when he was a Cadet Officer and I was a first year student. The one I will always remember most took place in December 1941. Through stupidity and a variety of misadventures I had piled up over 200 demerits and if these were not wiped out by Christmas vacation I would be expelled.

The school was closing for the holiday and that night the train would leave for home and I would not be coming back. "Ian's" father, Colonel J.M. Moore had asked one of the officer corps who lived in or near Lewisburg where the school was located to take charge of the "Beat", as the punishment was called. Needless to say, everyone wanted to start the

Christmas season but Cadet Lieutenant "Ian" Moore volunteered.

The snow was really swirling as we marched around the flag pole in front of the school. At the end of the first hour the other cadets had completed their hours and were released and left with a cry of joy as they headed home. I walked another hour and the snow was getting heavier and my heart was like a piece of led. After the second hour Lieutenant Moore told me to take a ten minute break, then return to walk in full dress uniform, overcoat and gloves. I thought, this was the ultimate to be expelled.

I reported back as ordered and the snow was coming down out of a sky turning dark. I had walked about two minutes when "Ian" called halt. He asked me if I saw the taxi parked by the front steps. I had not seen it drive up. "Cadet Cawley, the taxi will take you to the train station." His face lit up with a big smile." Have a wonderful Christmas and I'll see you in January." As the taxi pulled away I looked through the rear window and saw "Ian," alone in his cape, with the wind and snow whirling around him. He had just saved my academic life.

One of the greatest burdens than an individual can bear is to be the son of a famous father, no matter what his profession, and that doubles when your professional life follows in your father's footsteps. Think what it would be like in baseball if you were the son of Joe DiMaggio. Or football, if your father had been Joe Montana or Peyton Manning .

I have been at ringside and seen the second by second pressure of being Frank Sinatra Jr. Suppose you were George Patton, Jr. No matter how good you are there will always be people who will comment, "You're not as good as your old man." Critics spend a lifetime comparing their work with their father's and they will always be found wanting.

Although Liza has more than matched the career of her mother, Judy Garland, critics and fans will always add "but she's not the pure entertainer her mother was and God forbid that she ever sing "Over The Rainbow." It could never be as good as Judy.

The people I have mentioned have had it tough but nobody ever had it as tough as Joseph Marion "Ian" Moore. When Colonel J.M. Moore was President of Greenbrier and your father, it was impossible to excel enough to please. That "Ian" ever made Company Commander only speaks of his dedication to duty, his fantastic high grades, his athletic and military ability. I have no doubt that Colonel Joe fought every promotion every step of the way because in his mind "Ian" was still not good enough. Had he have stayed in school forever he would never have been Cadet Major and he was passed over for that post because he could never meet the impossible standards that the Colonel held. These were not the standards for the rest of the cadet corps ... but for his only son.

I thanked God every day that I did not have to meet his ultra-high standards. Although in the end, he met and conquered every one. Years later when I became a father I set what many thought were ultra-high standards for my children. My oldest daughter, Sharon met all those standards and excelled in every line of endeavor. It was too much for the other three, but then, they were not "Ian" Moore.

Upon graduation "Ian" was commissioned a Second Lieutenant in the U.S Army Infantry. He soon found himself in Europe as a member of General George Patton's hard-fighting army that was making the big push toward the invasion of Germany.

Everyone who knew "Ian" and the millions who didn't, saw his picture on the front page of almost every American newspaper when he received the Distinguished Service Cross from General George C. Marshall, Chief of Staff. The four-star General was on tour of the battle fronts in Europe.

Two weeks later as Patton's infantry pounded Axis defenses Lieutenant Moore found his platoon pinned down by German machine gun fire. The platoon was going to be wiped out, "Ian" followed the rules that all Greenbrier officers have been taught over and over again, "Follow Me." Never send men under you to do a job that you should do yourself. All alone, he charged the hill in the face of machine gun fire. He was wounded many times before he threw a packet of explosives into the bunker where the machine gun was located.

Second Lieutenant Joseph Marion "Ian" Moore sealed his duty with his life on that battle torn hill in Europe, saving a platoon of Patton's army that drove on to victory. Far from the sleepy little town of Lewisburg nestled in the rolling hills of southern West Virginia. He would have been the first to tell you that the leadership he provided was expected of all Greenbrier men and that what he did was nothing unusual.

"Ian" Moore's record as a cadet and a combat officer has the finest qualifications. In life and death he reached the highest standards of his country and his father. He is a true American hero.

THE MEDAL OF HONOR
BY
Robert Fregeau

Most Americans are aware that the Medal of Honor is our nation's highest award for valor while in uniform in the military service to the United States of America. But how many Americans know the history behind The Medal? Since its inception there have been nine versions of the medal.

The present-day medal began in 1847 as a Certificate of Merit authorized by the Congress and to be presented by the President of the United States to a "private soldier distinguish[ing] himself in the service", along with additional pay of $2 per month.

The first medal, known as the Navy Medal of Honor, was struck at the Philadelphia Mint for the Navy in 1862. The second design was for the Army, and was struck in 1862 from the original design with the exception that an eagle, crossed cannon and a saber replaced the anchor on the naval version of the medal.

In 1895, a change to the Army Medal of Honor was made that allowed for the wearing of a 'rosette', or ribbon in place of the Medal of Honor. Congress also allowed for a substitute red, white and blue ribbon to be used to replace deteriorating ribbons on the medal in 1896.

In 1904, the Congress authorized a new medal design which bore the now familiar blue ribbon with a field of thirteen stars. It was then known as the Gillespie Medal of Honor. Its designer, Brigadier General George Gillespie, was a recipient of the Medal of Honor from the Civil War.

The Tiffany Cross design of the Medal of Honor was implemented by the U.S. Navy for those deserving members who were in a Non-Combat role at the time of their heroism. Adopted by the Navy in 1919, it remained a valid award until its retirement in 1942.

Commencing with World War Two, the Medal of Honor design has morphed into its current configuration. It is no longer pinned to the tunic of the recipient; it is presented by the President of the United States by placing the blue ribbon over the head and around the neck of the recipient. In cases of posthumous presentation, it is presented by the president to the family in an oak and glass case.

Numerically, there has been only one female soldier awarded the Medal; a Civil War surgeon named Mary Edwards Walker. In 1917 her name was one of 911 Army Medal of Honor recipients deleted from the Roll. Her Medal was posthumously restored by then President Jimmy Carter in 1977.

Statistically, since the establishment of the Medal of Honor award, it has been issued to 3,458 recipients, of which eighty-five are currently living as of this narration. There have been nineteen double recipients of the Medal of Honor. There has not however, been a double recipient of the Medal of Honor since World War I. The first Medal of Honor was presented to Jacob Parrot, Private, United States Army on March 25, 1863. The most recent recipient is United States Marine Corps Sergeant Dakota Meyer. The Medal of Honor was presented to him on September 15, 2011 by President Obama.

In preparation for this report it must be noted that not all of the awardees of the Medal met the stellar qualities required for today's recipients. Several of the awards were made for such actions as the saving of the flag in combat. However, during the Civil War, no other award was available for presentation. Many of the medals awarded today can be seen as an elevation of the Medal of Honor for its true meaning of heroism and bravery. The criteria for the award of the Medal of Honor should always be the highest tradition of the service.

The term "hero" has received much use since September 11, 2001. In the context of this article, it is directed at the men and women of our military services who, through personal volition, have conducted themselves in a manner by which and for whom "all gave some, some gave all." For each recipient, it is their God and the Medal of Honor that continues to shine perpetual light upon them.

PATRIOTS AND HEROES

By

Jack Miller

I am a member of a small group of friends who are writers. Some are published authors while others are writing to become published. Keith Bettinger is a member, an author and a very sensitive man. He was a cop on the east coast and was involved in a traumatic incident. As a result, he became an expert in Post Traumatic Stress Disorder (PTSD). He has counseled others to get them over the hump, so to speak. Keith also loves being an American.

Recently he came up with an idea to do an anthology of patriotic stories with the members of this small group as the authors of this anthology. I found it a very interesting and exciting thought. I have always felt I was lucky to have been born in this great country and to be an American, so much so that I wanted to be part of such a project.

This project was apparently on my mind as I lay in bed waiting for sleep to overtake me, I began to think of patriots and heroes. Then I could not help but try to define the two. Was there a difference? I thought I knew, but then began to question what that difference was.

The next morning I broke out the dictionary:

Hero; any man admired for his courage, nobility or exploits especially in war.

Patriot: a person who loves and loyally or zealously supports his own country.

The last time I remember Americans as being patriotic was after the World Trade Center Towers being intentionally rammed by civilian airplanes which had been taken over and flown by terrorists on September 11, 2001. That feeling seemed to last for about thirty days, then began to wane before going back to normal. There were spurts of "Remember 9-11," but the solidarity of the American people against our attackers seemed to begin to subside after a month or so.

There was a time after December 7, 1941 when that patriotic solidarity was also present. But then, it lasted for years because the American people were involved. Kids collected newspapers, scrap iron and tin cans for recycling into war material. Ladies saved bacon grease and turned it in. Nylon was not available to civilians so ladies, in order to be stylish, painted a black stripe on the back of their bare legs so it appeared they were wearing nylon stockings. Men rushed to recruitment centers to volunteer for military service for the duration of the war plus six months. Convicted felons serving time in state prisons were volunteering to serve and were being accepted into the army. There was rationing of all types of food, especially coffee and sugar. Gasoline and tires were controlled items. People did not eat meat on Tuesdays or Fridays in order for those supplies to be made available to soldiers. Companies donated unused land so people could till, plant and grow vegetables in "Victory Gardens". Approximately 40% of what civilians ate came from these gardens.

Everyone heard the slogans and believed them; even lived them.

One of my favorites and one which our family lived by was "Use it up, wear it out. Make it do, or do without"

I had four older sisters and a younger brother. My dad, who had served in World War 1, was a Michigan State policeman, and was exempt from the draft. My three uncles all served voluntarily. Many homes, my grandparent's home included, proudly displayed a small banner in their front window. It was white with a red border. In the center was a blue star, one for each son or daughter serving in the military. Some people had a banner with as many as six blue stars. Sadly many of the flags also bore a gold star for each son or daughter killed in action during the war.

Most important was the self-censorship of the radio and newspapers. The War Department, asked the media not print information which might be helpful to the enemy such as ship movements, enlistments by name, military transfers or re-assignments; and even some successes of the military were not reported. In order to maintain support for the troops, reports of military failures or even just plain bad news was not made public. This was voluntarily enforced by editors, publishers and newscasters. Citizens remained in solid support of the war effort.

    I had correctly interpreted a hero as a person who did for other people, and a patriot who did for his country. That led me to more thoughts. The news media reports, almost daily, that some person in a mid-eastern country wearing a bomb blew up themselves and others for some religious cause. Are these people patriots or religious zealots? There are not too many around to ask why, so I guess each reader will have to judge and make up their own mind.

    So, it is my belief that a person can be a hero. A person can be patriotic. Some can be both, and are to be revered. Anyone who takes up the courage to serve should be honored to the utmost.

PRESIDENT'S DAY

By

Rena C. Winters

This past week, I found it difficult not to think about the President's holiday that we are soon celebrating. Lincoln was an outstanding President. Noted for being extremely fair minded. Washington, of course, the Father of Our Country certainly was a man of vision.

And my thoughts wandered to other countries I had visited. I remembered one day standing atop the Acropolis, a fortified hill in Athens, Greece, looking at the proud columned ruins of the Parthenon. One of the most magnificent of man's architectural creations, the Parthenon, was a Doric, which was a Greek religious temple centuries ago.

As I stood before it, I overhead an American marine comment, "I suppose the day will come when others will walk up the great stone steps to the ruins of the American White House and they will say,'Here once was a great civilization.'"

At Byblos, one of the oldest of the Middle East's many cities, one can stand and look through seven thousand years of history. One civilization built on the ruins of the last. There one sees the Stone Age and the civilizations of the Egyptians, the Phoenicians, the Babylonians, the Assyrians, the Greeks, the Arabs, the Romans, the Crusaders, and the Turks. One after another through seven thousand years empires rose and then fell from power.

Our history books speak of such colonial empires as Spain and Portugal in the Western Hemisphere. I know my grandmother, who came from Spain, would say "Don't forget in the past we ruled the world. Stand up straight, remember your manners, and act like a lady." None of which as a child I wanted to hear. However, at one time Spain was a very powerful country and now has greatly slipped from power. The Netherlands once ruled in the Far East and France once controlled Indochina. We have witnessed the decline of the British Empire, upon which it was once said, with understandable pride, "that the sun had never set."

Today, our nation, the USA, stamps its influence on world affairs. Mankind marvels at the technology that has put man on the moon and that probes into the far reaches of the solar system. Countries marvel at our wealth, our merchandise, our free institutions, our power.

And we, too, marvel and take pride in the works of our hands. We listen to the call of comfort, the allure of leisure, the demands and pleasures of power.

Better that we should listen thoughtfully to the wind that whispers sadly through the ruins of the Parthenon and observe the eternal stars that wink knowingly over the mounds of ancient cities. No nation is stronger than the ideals upon which it was built.

One nation. Are we really one nation, divided up into states, with different problems, different approaches to solving problems, to rectifying situations. For instance, such as allocation of funds for various projects. Why should some states have better medical programs for their people than others? Why should some states have better school programs than others? Perhaps it would be better if these things were considered on a national basis.

Under God. So much of our country today does not honor God. Or even acknowledge his existence. Much of our country is being purchased by foreigners with different ideals, different religious beliefs. They will begin to affect our national thinking. Our economic planning, and those with no religious beliefs certainly will, and do now affect our country's moral standing. Frequently people with no religious beliefs are those that also do not honor any laws or practice acceptable standards of behavior.

Indivisible. Today we see riots in the streets, various protests of all types. I wonder, are we trying to ban together, or separate those that do not agree with us? Aren't we really dividing, instead of multiplying? We should be multiplying our strengths, and finding our common goals and ambitions for our country. Indivisible? I don't really know. I have to say honestly it worries me, what I see happening in American today.

No nation is stronger than the ideals upon which it was built, and when those ideals are forgotten, so also shall the nation be forgotten. Until someday a citizen of some yet unknown land, be it from another country, or from outer space, shall stand and ponder the glory that once was "one nation indivisible, under God, with freedom and justice for all.

I want with all my heart to believe that our nation is the greatest and that it will always be. Yet one has to wonder.

Does history repeat itself?

Can we wake up in time to see the problems?

Do enough people really care about their country anymore?

Let's join together in thinking about our nation. Under God, indivisible with freedom and justice for all and how we as an individual can help. Can we do our part? Become more involved? Support our country?

Radical, yes I am about the United States being the greatest.

Angry, yes about what I see going on; protests, anti American tolerance.

Worried, yes, because I love my country.

American, yes and very proud of it.

RICHARD ALLEN KERR

A True Hero

By

Robert Cawley

Richard Kerr was a native of Pennsylvania, the same state that produced Charles E. "Commando" Kelly of Medal Of Honor fame. Richard was known for his sense of humor and artistic talents and was an excellent cartoonist. After he graduated from Greenbrier Military School in 1946 he enlisted in the Marine Corps.

He moved up in rank in a rapid period of time. He became a sergeant and squad leader of a rifle platoon during the Korean war. For his leadership and valor in combat, he was awarded the Silver Star.

After Korea, he served as a recruiting officer, Naval ROTC instructor and was promoted to the rank of master sergeant. Later he was designated a Marine gunner, a Warrant Officer qualified for command of a tactical unit.

In the late 1950's Richard became a Chief Warrant Officer and was commissioned a Second Lieutenant. This ambitious young man completed flight training and was designated a Radar Intercept Officer, flying in the back seat of a F-4 Phantom Jet where he logged over 1,000 hours of flight time.

He was sent to Vietnam and assigned to Marine Fighter Attack Squadron 323. While serving in Vietnam he was awarded 10 Air Medals for 213 combat missions flown against Viet Cong and North Vietnamese targets.

Richard Allen Kerr was killed on January 31, 1968, when the Marine Corps airfield at Chu Lai, Republic of Vietnam, came under attack.

Richard Kerr was inducted into the Greenbrier Military Alumni Hall Of Fame in 2008 not due to losing his life while serving his country, but for the way he served his country while he lived. He was a true hero.

A FOOT AHEAD

By

Charles McKee

My year and a half as a stock boy during my junior and senior year in High School was a learning experience to say the very least.

The shock of working with a one on one supervisor was different, and very busy. "Mac" kept me busy from the first day I was assigned to the delivery dock. As a matter of fact, my first eighty carton delivery found him seated on the delivery trucks bumper smoking a cigarette while the driver and I made a quick count.

Needless to say, I survived the hard work, and more than earned my dollar and ten cents per hour wage. This is also the time when I learned to take a lunch rather that spend the half hour walking to a nearby restaurant and using up nearly an hour's wage, plus shoe leather.

Seven months after high school graduation, found me earning seventy- eight dollars a month while serving aboard a United States Navy destroyer.

Upon my return in the early nineteen sixties, I found job hunting difficult to say the least. While my navy salary topped at one hundred twenty dollars a month; with sea pay, it had also included a "grey bed" and breakfast with short vacations.

My job hunting brought me back to the JC Penney store in my home town in Richmond, California. The store was at 8th and MacDonald Streets smack dab in the busy part of the city I grew up in.

The only spot available was shoe salesman. The store was open six days a week, and the shoe department maintained seven employees. They also had three of us part time workers who attended a local junior college.

Mr. Walter Jenny, department manager, conducted the business of the shoe department as if it were his own store. We would all soon learn the methods of his guidance and motivation.

The boss drove a 1935 Chevrolet to work each day, and the car itself spoke volumes of its owner. It was brown, a compact business coupe, and it always seemed to move slowly and distinctly. It was Mr. Walter Jenny with wheels.

This man was a hero and friend to all that knew him. He offered spirited conversation, direct supervision, and motivated each of us in the area of sales that I had never heard of. This gentleman loved his job, loved the Penney product, loved all of his employees, and loved the United States of America.

The detective that conducted the background interview for my Oakland Police Officer position provided observations regarding me that I never heard, nor knew that existed.

This man is one of my life's Heroes, and what he imparted to me as a young worker lives with me today. His training was so utterly complete that the company offered my sales buddy John Lehman, and I positions as store management trainees.

Well done Mr. Walter Jenny; I doubt that you truly know how many employee and customer lives you touched while living your own.

BURIED ALIVE

By

Robert Fregeau

There can be no greater horror than to be buried alive. On September 11, 2001 thousands of Americans in both New York City and Washington D.C. either lived or died having experienced the process of being buried alive.

What goes through the mind of a human being at that point? Let's ask one human being who was pulled from the depths of one of the World Trade Center towers on a day we have come to express and revere as "Nine-Eleven."

In his capacity as a New York/New Jersey Port Authority Police Officer, Sergeant McLoughlin was on duty several miles from the carnage in progress at the World Trade Center complex. There was no hesitation, his duty was clear. He quickly formed a team of officers including a rookie, Will Jimeno.

After suiting up in their appropriate rescue gear, the officers entered a passageway connecting the Twin Towers. Moments later the South Tower exploded and crashed with such brutal force, it immediately killed two members of McLoughlin's team. He recalled "Initially, I thought I was dead. I had no sense of sight, smell or sound." A third officer in his group, Dominick Pezullo had managed to free himself from the initial collapse and was attempting to rescue his team members when he was struck and killed by a piece of falling debris from the North Tower.

The remaining officers, McLoughlin and Jimeno were in close proximity to each other. Each in his own way, made mental and verbal communications for what they believed they would have to accept...being buried alive in the rubble of the World Trade Center.

Jason Thomas, former Sergeant, United States Marine Corps and veteran of *Operations Iraqi Freedom* and *Enduring Freedom* in Afghanistan was in civilian status on September 11, 2001. His mother had just informed him of the disaster that had unfolded at the World Trade Center. Without hesitation, [Sgt.] Thomas donned his BDU uniform and proceeded to the site. On arrival he witnessed the collapse of Tower Two and he ran toward the ashen cloud racing toward him. His only thought was "*Someone needs help and I have the training to do it.*"

Jason Thomas assisted by fighting fires, helping survivors of the fallen WTC and comforting the dying. He subsequently met another former Marine, Staff Sergeant Dave Karnes. Karnes, likewise a veteran of *Operations Desert Storm and Iraqi Freedom* had come from Connecticut with some rescue gear. Searching through the rubble, they heard what would later be described as "muffled calls for help." They instructed the trapped victims to continue yelling in order to pinpoint their location. Thomas went on to attract the attention of additional rescue workers who aided in the extraction of the trapped and injured men.

Sergeant John McLoughlin and Officer Will Jimeno were saved from being buried alive by volunteer rescuers Jason Thomas and Dave Karns. Heroes all; they command the respect of a very grateful nation. By the way, did I mention that Sergeant John McLoughlin was the last survivor to be pulled from the World Trade Center?

ERIC DIXON'S FOURTH OF JULY

By

Keith Bettinger

It is July 4, 2006. The weather is strange – hot and sticky and windless, not what you become use to in the desert of Las Vegas. Lately the news has not been pleasant regarding the war in Iraq, the bickering of politicians in Washington, and threats of violence and nuclear activities worldwide. In towns across our country, ears are assaulted by rap music and graffiti defaces property in both affluent and poor communities. Where are the youth of the United States going? Where are they taking us? Are these really the people who are going to lead this country as the next generation takes over? Today I found out not only am I becoming one of those grumpy senior citizens who worries too much about the future, I also learned that some of these young people truly are the leaders of the next generation, and that we can be very proud of them.

A few days ago, I heard a Las Vegas radio commentator talking about the efforts of a seventeen-year-old Las Vegan, Eric Dixon, who undertook a very special project to attain his Eagle Scout award in the Boy Scouts of America. The commentator said that Eric would be placing American Flags in the park located at Lone Mountain and Durango in

Las Vegas to honor the over two thousand five hundred service people who died in the war in Iraq.

When my friend and I arrived at the park, we saw that Eric, his family and his scoutmaster had placed three hundred and twenty-four flags on a gentle rise in the park. The flags were evenly spaced as if they were standing at attention on a field of honor. Each flagpole had a tag containing the names of at least eight service people. Each tag was individually typed, containing the name, rank, branch of service and the specifics about how and when each service person died. Some of the flagpoles had yellow or red ribbons tied to them – remembering someone who was lost — red for Clark County, yellow for the State of Nevada.

I walked amongst the flags reading some of the tags — male and female, officer and enlisted ranks, Army, Navy, Air Force and Marines, all were remembered and homage paid. There was a stillness there — a respectful silence. People walked amongst the flags including the parents of a fallen Marine who left them behind when he was only eighteen years old. They stood proudly by the flag that contained his name and that of seven other American heroes. My friend and I watched them from a distance as we let them have their time with their son.

Eric explained why he took on this project. He wanted these heroes to be remembered and he did this by following the rules and guidelines for Eagle Scout projects. He requested assistance from businesses, organizations and members of the community. One local union gave him the pieces of rebar cut to size to hold the flagpoles. A landscaping company gave him PVC pipes to use as flagpoles, and a large home store gave him end caps to finish off the PVC flagpoles. A friend of the family built a tool to drive the rebar six inches into the ground, so the flags and their poles could proudly stand in the park. Businesses and members of the community contributed money to buy the flags. It was nice to see that some of the names of the donors were from foreign lands – people who moved here to find a better life. They knew this was a way to say thank you to those who made it possible for them to live in this country.

As I prepared to leave this special place, I took one more look at the flags. A strong breeze came up causing all the flags to stand straight out as if they were coming to attention and saying thank you for visiting with us.

Eric deserves his promotion to Eagle Scout, but more importantly, he deserves the recognition of the public. He is a future leader of this community and an asset to this country. The world will be a better place in the future when we leave it in the hands of young American citizens like Eric Dixon.

I AM AN AMERICAN AND PROUD OF IT

By

Jack Miller

We fought two wars on our soil. First was the war for independence from England. Winning that, our next war was a civil war over the rights of states to allow slavery or to enforce a sentence in the Declaration of Independence wherein "all Men are created equal, that they are endowed by their Creator with certain unalienable rights, that among these are Life, Liberty, and the Pursuit of Happiness." (sic) Although many Americans who wore either blue or grey died for their beliefs, I am happy and agree with the outcome.

Some people smuggle themselves into the United States of America. Some enter legally. Some retain their foreign citizenship, while others give up loyalty to their homeland and swear allegiance to the United States of America and become citizens.

I'm one of the lucky ones. I didn't have to do any of that – I was born an American.

I'm fortunate in that I am an American. I'm proud of that. I'm not a Scottish-American; an Anglo- American, an

Irish-American, a French-American or a German-American, although I am all of these. I am, pure and simple, an American.

I have been from my birth in 1935.

I have never been ashamed of America, although at times I wish our legislators did things differently. But that is one of the things that make me a proud American; I have the right to disagree.

America has fed the hungry, healed the sick, and freed the enslaved of other countries. We gave of our wealth and our health. We never took the spoils of war. We never forced our beliefs upon the people or countries we fought and won over. The only thing we asked for was a piece of hallowed ground so we could bury Americans who died for others. I agree with that, but have to disagree with the way we have treated some of our own Americans.

Americans have developed cures or vaccines for diseases, and then given them free to the world. I agree with that. But then some of those cures and vaccines have not been made available to our own, except at very high prices that not everyone can afford. I disagree with that.

We have provided arms and ammunition to citizens of other countries who have wanted to change their own oppressive governments. We have offered training to these citizens so they might have a better chance of surviving the enemies they overthrow. I agree that this is the right thing to do, however, I disagree with leaving the arms and ammunition with them after they become successful in their endeavor. Too often, the new government becomes corrupt and turns those same guns and ammunition against us.

I disagree with giving money to other countries which are better off than we are, or that treat us as enemies.

It is my right to publically disagree. It is my right to publically say I disagree. These are some of my rights as an American.

Our forefathers fought for and won these and other rights for us.

I do not agree with what some people within our borders claim. Some black Americans refer to themselves as "African Americans." Others refer to themselves as "Spanish-Americans," "Chinese- Americans," "Mexican- Americans," and the list goes on. To be proud of your heritage is good, and to remember your roots is a benefit to that, but, we should all just be Americans.

On Dec 7, 1941, and again on Sep 11, 2001, the American people were attacked. Foreign enemies brought a war to our soil. They made the initial blow, but not the final blow. The American people banded together against a common enemy. Both events predicated the use of military force against the attackers. We took the fight to them rather than fight them on our shores. I agree with that.

I believe we should get back to the basics. I believe we should always remember we are Americans. We live in the greatest country in the world. We should all be proud to call ourselves Americans, and we should conduct ourselves as proud Americans.

I MET A HERO TODAY

By

Marshal Taylor

When I was in college, I opposed the Vietnam War. However, I had done a hitch in the regular Army, and if I had been sent to Vietnam, I would have gone. I probably would have also gotten myself killed, since my record for getting eliminated in war games was pretty much 100%.

But that's not what I wanted to tell you about. Even though I was against the war, and even protested against it, I never was against the troops that got sent there. Just as I don't think we should have gone into Iraq, I don't think we should have gone into Vietnam. We wasted valuable lives and squandered treasure in both cases. But that's all hindsight.

It was after the war was over that I learned about how some stupid people had jeered at troops coming home. Quite truthfully, it made me sick and if I had witnessed any of that, I would have punched someone out, but I wasn't where things like that were happening.

Today, I saw a car with a sticker that said the owner was a member of the "Association of Tunnel Rats." Tunnel Rats were the soldiers who went down into the Viet Cong tunnels to fight the enemy on their own terms. Sometimes the tunnels were dark, sometimes they were booby-trapped, and they were often home to poisonous snakes and spiders.

The gentleman I spoke to was an older Polynesian man, who was missing a lot of his teeth. He had a grey beard, which was long enough so that he could have combed it over the bald spot on his head; sort of the reverse of what Donald Trump does. The man was about five foot nine or so, and maybe close to two hundred pounds; in other words, stocky.

We talked for a while about what he had done in the war. I mentioned that I thought the tunnel guys were smaller than he was, and he laughed when he told me he used to be very skinny. But then he turned sad and told me how much it had hurt when people railed against him and his buddies after they came home. He was still hurt and angry about that treatment even after thirty-five years or so.

I told him that I had been RA (Regular Army, a term used to identify volunteers who served a three year enlistment as opposed to draftees who served two years); that I had gotten out before Vietnam; that I had protested the war; but had never protested the soldiers who had to fight. I told him that I admired what he had done, and that I was sorry he and his fellows had been so poorly treated. We parted after that, he with his Starbucks coffee and me with my thoughts.

After all those years, this man is still carrying the weight of the tunnels without any real appreciation for the job he had to do. I cannot imagine what dreams and nightmares such a man has, and I'm not sure I would want to know. What I do know is that I met a hero this morning, and I wish I could have said something to make up for the years he has felt sad about his homecoming. Somehow, I don't think anything I said would have been enough. Maybe I did as much as I could do by saying thank you.

THOMAS EDGAR "JOCK" CLIFFORD

By

Robert M. Cawley

They have little time for glory in the infantry but every soldier in World War II has to have a special place in their heart for a fighting colonel who led his men and died in the service of his country.

A native of Ronceverte, West Virginia and a graduate of Greenbrier Military School, Class of 1932 "Jock" fulfilled the early promise he gave on Greenbrier's playing fields and the United States Military Academy at West Point when he was selected first-team All-American center in 1935.

At West Point, as an honor student, he was a master of academics. A standout in journalism he was Editor In Chief of The Pointer. He excelled as a rifle marksman, pistol marksman and was a member of the Lecture Committee. Off the gridiron he proved his athletic ability in Soccer and Fencing. The same characteristics which gained him renown in athletics gained him national acclaim as a battlefield leader in World War II.

He graduated from West Point in 1936 and was assigned to the 24th Infantry Division in Hawaii where he fought against the Japanese attack on Pearl Harbor.

He moved on with the division when it was transferred to Australia and when they saw their first action in New Guinea in 1944 Clifford was a Lt. Colonel and Commander of the 21st Infantry. He led the battalion during that campaign and won the Silver Star following the capture of Hollandin Airdrome. Throughout the entire period of this operation, often under heavy enemy fire, he distinguished himself by gallantry in action above and beyond the call of duty showing complete disregard for his personal safety in order to accomplish his mission.

At the battle of Leyte his aggressive leadership and courageous personal conduct in close combat with the enemy, imbued his men with an indomitable fighting spirit, the direct result being the defeat of the enemy. He led a brilliant dash by his battalion around Japanese defenses and took and held Kilay Ridge fighting off ten Japanese attacks over twenty-four days. His battalion received the Presidential Citation for this action and Clifford was awarded his first Distinguished Service Cross.

Promoted to full Colonel "Jock" took command of the 19th Infantry Regiment which was picked as an assault regiment and they surged across Mindoro, Luzon and Mindanao then drove to capture Davao City in what was called "One of the most brilliantly executed coups by any regiment in the Pacific area." On June 24, 1945 Colonel Clifford was killed during a mortar attack near Tamogan, Mindanao.

After his death a junior office was quoted saying: "Over and above all the men and their hardships, there stood the forceful and dominating personality of our commander. I doubt if any man has ever done more than him to keep his men fighting and holding on by the sheer weight of his personal leadership."

Two awards of the Distinguished Service Cross, a Silver Star, a Legion of Merit, a Bronze Star and a Purple Heart are his military honors. The National Guard Armory in Ronceverte, West Virginia, a small arms range at Fort Stewart, Georgia, and the town square in Davao, Philippine Islands are named in his honor.

No finer soldier ever wore the uniform of our army. No braver commander ever led his unit to battle. He was not only a skillful and gifted soldier but the kind of military man we would all like to be.

Student, athlete, soldier, husband, father, Thomas Edgar "Jock" Clifford, Jr.... A VERY SPECIAL MAN.

"Jock" was inducted into the Greenbrier Military School Sports Hall Of Fame in 1996.

HEROES, PATRIOTS AND VICTIMS

By

Jack Miller

We know of the destruction of the Twin Towers in New York on September 11, 2001. We know of those who worked in the towers and were able to get out. We also know of the thousands who were unable to get out and became victims. We know the attack was made by Muslim extremists who became victims themselves. We know of the heroic actions by firemen and policemen who entered the burning towers to save people some of whom became victims of that destruction.

There were many heroes and victims that day. But, but there were also some patriots. There were several patriots aboard flight 93, the one that ended in a field with no survivors. That plane had some heroes and patriots who also became victims. One of the ones we know of was a man named Todd Beamer. He uttered the now famous words, "Let's Roll!"

I don't think I would want to utter the words "Let's Roll" during a skyjacking, but I believe I would, given similar circumstances. I am 77 years old and in reasonable health; and I have some strength which I feel I would use to attempt to subdue anyone who was trying to take over my life and the lives of others. I know there are others who feel the same. The big problem is we do not have a plan worked out or a signal to execute the plan should we ever find ourselves in a hi-jacking.

Neither did Todd Beamer, as a passenger on United Flight 93, on September 11, 2001. He did not want to have to fight back, but he and others did. In the investigation of the incident, it appeared that Beamer and several others had been seated together in the back of the plane by one of the four sky-jackers. While the terrorist was away from where they were seated the men discussed overcoming the high-jackers. It appeared that Beamer and the others fought back in a hastily designed plan to attempt to save the passengers and crew. What they did not know was that the pilot and co-pilot had been murdered and the plane was piloted by a terrorist to be used as a bomb and crash into, investigators believe, the U.S. Capitol. "Let's Roll" were the last words anyone on the ground would hear Todd Beamer say.

Since 9-11, the airlines have had their cockpit doors reinforced to prevent takeovers. Sky marshals fly on some aircraft. We are now inconvenienced with searches, examinations, and a lot of rules and restrictions by TSA when we fly.

Even with the increased security, terrorists can attempt to take over areas filled with people, be it, a sporting event, bus or even a restaurant. We as freedom loving people must be prepared emotionally and mentally to fight back. We must recognize that some might get hurt or even die. However, the odds are we would only be injured. Gunshots are more apt to injure than to kill. However, to allow terrorists to continue with their plans, whatever that they may be, will surely kill all everyone or at least a great many. If I am in a circumstance where I am probably going to die anyway, I would rather die a hero than a coward.

If faced with a terrorist takeover, I would hope that all men and women have the same plan. It is not a time to be concerned with political correctness, gentleness or even moral niceness. Tackle the terrorist, hold onto an arm, a leg or a neck. Gouge their eyes, grab and squeeze their scrotum until it brings tears to their eyes. If a female, do not be afraid to grab them by the breast and squeeze until it hurts them. Get them on the ground. Step on the wrist or the hand holding a weapon while the others kick or choke the terrorist into unconsciousness. The objective must be to neutralize the threats at all costs. By overtaking the terrorist you will be saving lives. As the saying goes, it is better to be judged by twelve than carried by six.

Terrorists in a takeover scenario have most always herded their captives together to be more easily guarded by one or two terrorists. Be ready to act before that or at least during that phase. As soon as the people understand they are being forced into a takeover situation, all those who are able and willing to act should move to get close to the terrorists.

There must be a signal amongst the heroes and I suggest the "V" for victory sign made famous by Sir Winston Churchill. Once it is known that there are others with a like mind willing to take the chance, they must strike. Next, a signal needs to be agreed upon as a standard signal to initiate the action. Why not keep the last know words of Hero, Patriot and Victim, Todd Beamer our rally signal, "Let's Roll."

    Many takeovers (high-jacking's) heinous acts have started with the terrorist getting everyone's attention by yelling, showing weapons, making threats and committing violent acts. Often a hand grenade or a dead man switch is used. Not everyone knows how these devices operate and how to neutralize them. Most grenades used are the small hand held type. The fuse for these is screwed into the grenade. The grenade without a fuse is inert. To activate the fuse, the cotter pin has to be pulled and the handle, or spoon, must be released. When released, the spoon will fly away allowing a spring loaded striker to engage a firing pin which will slowly burn down the fuse taking several seconds before the grenade will explode. If the terrorist is gripping a grenade by the handle, try to get the grenade away without allowing the handle to be released. This is easiest if the large metal ring is still attached to the cotter pin which holds the spoon. If not, grip the grenade and the handle and wrest it away while holding the handle. If the spoon is still attached but the pin pulled, insert a bobby pin, or a ballpoint pen ink cartridge or anything strong and stiff into the hole at the top of the spoon. This should render the grenade safe, but place it safely down and leave it alone. If when you are overpowering the terrorist and the pin is out and the handle has flown off, try your best to roll the terrorist onto the armed grenade and wait for the explosion. If that is impossible, as quickly as you can throw the grenade into a restroom and close the door or if that is not possible throw it to where the least number of people are. That will damage the airplane and could cause it to crash but what are the options, really? If you are on the ground and there is a dumpster available, use it. If the terrorist is holding a dead man's switch, his thumb or fore finger will be pressing down on a button. As long as the button is held down the device is safe. Try to keep his digit on the button or force it aside keeping the button depressed. Then you may either keep holding the button or use tape to keep pressure on it.

Homeland security is not just the responsibility of the airlines, TSA or the sky marshals, nor is it just the responsibility of the police departments across the nation. There are situations where we must take some matters into our own hands. We must be prepared to fight and recognize that we may get hurt in the process, but our freedoms have never been free. They have been paid for in blood by the military, the police and citizens. Now, that torch has been passed to us, it might be our turn. Remember, a cut can be sutured and a gunshot seldom kills. With a "V" for victory over any terrorists trying to kill us we can win. Now "Let's Roll."

LOST AND FOUND

By

Keith J. Bettinger

On November 18, 1918, the Great War was over for one whole week. People who had lost hope suddenly found a reason to be happy again. Their soldiers would soon return home. New York City was in the middle of an Indian summer with a record setting temperature of sixty-eight degrees. The New York Times consisted of twenty-four pages of news and ads. The advertisements in the newspaper announced a sale on men's suits from twenty-five to sixty-five dollars at the exclusive Saks Fifth Avenue department store. The New York Times sold for the sum of two cents.

Patrolman Thomas Gilbert, shield number 6595, a member of the New York City Police Department, reported for duty that day. He was a widower with five children; three sons, Thomas, William and Harold, and two daughters, Margaret and Helen. The day did not seem any different for him. Peace was already one week old. His son, William, serving in the American Expeditionary Forces was now safe. Life on the streets of Manhattan remained the same. Gilbert was assigned to traffic duty in the heart of Manhattan, Times Square, at 42nd Street. It was the same duty he had been assigned to for years. When his duty was done, he would return home and find children waiting to greet him just like any other day.

Thomas Gilbert was busy doing what he did every day, directing traffic in the middle of the intersection. Directing traffic in those days was just as dangerous as it is today. Traffic in New York City was heavy even in 1918. The traffic's orderly flow was controlled by police officers. While standing in the intersection, Patrolman Gilbert was struck by an errant vehicle. People rushed to his aid, but Patrolman Gilbert died. He was lost. He was lost to the city that employed him. He was lost to his friends with whom he worked. Most importantly, he was lost to his children, just one day before his daughter Helen's fourteenth birthday and two days before his own fiftieth birthday.

After the funeral, time went on for the rest of the world. Patrolman Gilbert joined officers lost before his own passing. Later on, somewhere in the expanse of eternity, other officers joined him and his fellow celestial police officers. Many of those that joined him had died in the line of duty. However, for some reason or circumstance, his sacrifice was lost in the vast history of the New York City Police Department. He was forgotten by all but his family.

The cohesiveness of the Gilbert family was lost as well. The sons were too old to receive their father's pension benefits. His pension money went to Margaret and Helen until each one became eighteen years old. Then like their father, the benefits were gone. His son, Thomas, left the city and started a life of his own. Margaret and Helen were sent to boarding school. For many years, they thought the police department was taking care of their education and needs. Only later in life did they find out an anonymous benefactor paid for their education and care. When William returned from the war, he followed in his father's footsteps. He too, became a New York City Police Officer.

In May of 1997, Guy Painter was a sergeant with the Los Angeles Airport Police. He was speaking to his friend and coworker, Police Officer Darren Gilbert. During the conversation, Darren said his great-grandfather was a New York City Patrolman who was killed while directing traffic. Darren did not know any other details about the death of his Great-grandfather. In order to learn more details, Guy checked the National Law Enforcement Officers Memorial directory. He was unable to find Patrolman Gilbert's name listed anywhere on the Memorial.

Without saying anything to Darren, Guy wrote to the National Law Enforcement Officers Memorial. He inquired as to why Patrolman Gilbert had never been included in the roll call of fallen officers. The Memorial staff searched their records and found that the New York City Police Department never forwarded Patrolman Thomas Gilbert's name to be included on the Memorial. Somewhere in the bureaucracy he remained lost and forgotten.

Without the Gilbert family's knowledge, Guy persisted in his endeavor to have Patrolman Gilbert's name placed on the national memorial. He wrote to the New York City Police Department. His mail was forwarded through channels to the Chief of Personnel. The Chief of Personnel was surprised to read that a fallen officer was missing from the department's honor roll. He assigned a detective to investigate the matter.

In the beginning of February 1998, Guy received a phone call at his office. A New York City Police Department detective, who was assigned the investigation by the Chief of Personnel, had information for Guy regarding his inquiry. She informed Guy that the investigation was completed and it was ascertained that Patrolman Thomas Gilbert did indeed die in the line of duty. The facts of the case had been forwarded to Police Commissioner Howard Safir in January of 1998 for his review. Commissioner Safir read the investigation file. He approved the change of status noting that Patrolman Gilbert died in the line of duty. The Commissioner ordered Patrolman Gilbert's name to be added to the Memorial in the lobby of One Police Plaza. The date for that honor was scheduled for the annual memorial service that would be held during May 1998. The detective also told Guy, Commissioner Safir had forwarded Patrolman Gilbert's name and records to the New York State Police Memorial in Albany. Patrolman Gilbert would also be honored at the State Ceremony in Albany in May 1998, following the New York City ceremony.

Unfortunately, the process for inclusion on memorials is long and arduous. Because each memorial has different criteria and each case must be investigated, Patrolman Gilbert was not included in the 1998 National Memorial Service in

Washington. The detective was sorry that the investigation was completed too late for Patrolman Gilbert to be considered for the National Memorial Service. The detective advised Guy that the New York City Police Department already submitted Patrolman Gilbert's name to the National Memorial Committee. The department had been assured that Patrolman Gilbert's name would be added to the National Memorial at Judiciary Square in Washington, D.C. on May 13, 1999. On behalf of Commissioner Safir, she thanked Guy for bringing the omission to the department's attention. She advised him that copies of all the documents would be sent to him. She then asked if he would do the honor of informing the Gilbert family of Patrolman Gilbert's inclusion on the memorials. Guy gladly accepted the task.

About one week later, the package of documents, addressed to Guy, arrived at the Los Angeles Airport Police stationhouse. Guy and his Captain got together and conspired on how to give Darren the news. They ordered Darren into the Captain's office. Darren looked around with a worried look upon his face. It was a look that asked, "What did I do now?" Guy told Darren to take a seat.

When Darren was seated, Guy told him a matter of great importance had come to their attention and it needed to be addressed. Guy handed him the correspondence from the New York City Police Department. Darren read it and was at a loss for words. His great-grandfather was no longer lost. His records, his history and his sacrifice had been found.

In May of 1998, Darren Gilbert traveled to New York. He and the rest of the surviving Gilbert family journeyed to One Police Plaza. There in a sea of New York City Police Department uniforms, stood one officer, in the dress uniform of the Los Angeles Airport Police. Darren and the Gilbert family saw Thomas Gilbert honored for his sacrifice as his name was added to the department's honor role.

In May of 1999, Darren went to Washington, DC. On the evening of May 13, during the Candlelight Vigil, he heard his great-grandfather's name read with those of other fallen heroes. Thomas Gilbert's name was added to a place of honor amongst fifteen thousand other names. Thomas Gilbert's name found the place it so rightfully deserved on Panel 25 West, Line 21.

Guy Painter, who is now a lieutenant, was not able to make the trips to honor the officer he worked so hard to find. As often happens in police work, duty and manpower allocations do not allow an officer the time he needs to fulfill his personal goals. However, rewards for jobs well done do come in many different forms. On the wall of his office, prominently displayed for everyone to see, is a framed handwritten letter from Darren's aunt, Patrolman Gilbert's granddaughter. It is a heartfelt sentiment; thanking Guy for all that he did to honor Patrolman Thomas Gilbert. It is a special gift that has not been lost on Guy. It has found a special place in his heart.

MEMORIES IN GREEN:

Recollections of Martha "Maggie" Raye

By

Charles McKee

Let me be the first to acknowledge another review of one of the most revered and loved women in the history of the United States Military. Searching for information on an American icon is sometimes a difficult task, to say the very least. This was not the case with Martha Raye. Much of my success in this writing is attributed to Maggie's friend and acclaimed author Noonie Fortin, who wrote MEMORIES OF MAGGIE.

As a youngster, I watched Martha Raye and her accentuated wide mouth and uproarious comedic style in both television and film. If you didn't laugh at Martha Raye, your giggle box must have been turned off. It is indeed a shame that many of we Americans lack her style, grace and patriotism. Maggie was an American first, and stage performer second. She dedicated her life to the American GI, and paid her dues as a card carrying supporter of all American military personnel that found themselves in combat throughout the second world war, Korean war and of course the Vietnam war.

Maggie is by no means the only entertainer that volunteered to enter a theater of combat operations to entertain our troops. Names like Bob Hope, Connie Stevens, Jerry Colonna, Wayne Newton, Joey Heatherton, Gary Sinise, Jack Jones and many others have pledged their own time; and assumed personal risk to be of service to American military personnel engaged in combat, and far from their homes and loved ones.

"Maggie" was actually born Margy Reed, in St. James Hospital, Butte, Montana, on the twenty seventh day of August, 1916. She changed her name to Martha Raye some years later. Martha's parents, Maybelle and Pete had two additional children; Melodye and Bud.

There are some rumors regarding Martha Raye and her many accomplishments, but, we do know that she did not finish the fifth grade; nor, was she a nurse. Although, Maggie was rumored to have performed many nursing skills in emergency settings while in Viet Nam.

Maggie did however, receive some training as a *Candy Striper* sometime in the 1930's. It would be obvious that Martha was going to serve her fellow men in each and every opportunity presented to her.

In Bob Hope's book, *"Five Women I Love"* (Double Day Press); Bob Remarks: "My friend Jonny Grant was in Vietnam taping interviews with GI's; and there was Martha Raye. Martha had already been in Viet Nam for about three weeks, thumbing airlifts to the remotest bases." There she was, just Martha and a couple of musicians. "What am I talking about, not a big show?"

When you've got Martha, you don't need anything else.

On Mr. Hope's first contact with Martha Raye, he didn't recognize her. She was clad in Viet Nam era combat fatigues, combat boots and a floppy green fatigue hat to block out the constant Viet Nam heat and sun. She is said to have worn the silver oak leaves of a US Army Lieutenant Colonel. And Bob was quoted as saying "The newspaper stories were true… Martha was really a Colonel… God help the Cong!"

As I mentioned earlier, may rumors have been told regarding the GI's great friend and entertainer, Martha Raye. Martha was apparently not afraid of danger as she often showed up at US Army Special Forces camps far from the safety of large numbers of US troops. It is also rumored that during a performance, the Camp was attacked and she was rushed to safety. That was not Colonel "Maggie's" style. It has been reported that she was seen engaging the enemy with one of the Camps heavy M2-50 caliber machine guns.

The US Army Special Forces adopted her, and she was often seen wearing the Green Beret of US Army "Special Forces." On one occasion I observed her Green Beret Flash patch sporting the Eagle emblem of a full Coronel of Special Forces. She was of course an honorary member of the Green

Berets; and I am sure "her" troops would insist the emphasis be made on the word "honor."

Where does the United States find such people of this caliber? Martha Raye, Bob Hope; and a host of other famous heroic and patriotic Americans are just a few of those that must be counted amidst our heroic listings. And thanks to current day heroes like Gary Sinise, Wayne Newton and many others; who still support our troops in combat wherever they may be serving.

On the nineteenth of October, 1994, the United States lost a true American hero and patriot. Martha "Maggie" Raye; the little girl from Butte, Montana died; And even in her passing there were more rumors. Where is our hero truly buried? Not in Arlington National Cemetery as thought; but in the United States Army Special Forces Cemetery, gravesite number 780-B in Fort Bragg ,North Carolina.

Rest in peace our American hero and patriot.

OUR MONUMENT AT LAST

By

Keith Bettinger

On October 15, 1991, American Law Enforcement Officers and their families finally received their reward for honor, duty, courage and sacrifice. October 15th saw thousands of people in the confines of Judiciary Square, in Washington, D.C., for the dedication of the National Law Enforcement Officers Memorial.

Love and thought went into the design of the "Wall" as some call it. The monument is made of light grey marble. The names of 12,561 law enforcement officers killed in the line of duty between 1794 and 1990 are randomly listed on the wall. The wall is divided into panels that are numbered one to sixty-three, both east and west. There is a continuous bench opposite the walls of names, so survivors and friends can sit and visit with their officer.

If you are looking for a loved one, it is easy to find their name. At each of the two entrances, there are two books listing officers alphabetically. If you are looking for someone from a particular department, the rear of the book is edited by state, then department, and then officer, date of death, the panel number, and the line of names on the panel.

The monument is beautiful, both day and night. During the day, the symmetrically shaped trees, evenly spaced gardens, and manicured lawn add dignity and beauty to the fountain. There are two flagpoles, one displaying a large American Flag, and the other the Memorial Flag. The Memorial Flag has a blue shield with a rose on a white background, encased in red and gold. During the evening, the flags fly, fully lighted. The names on the wall can be easily read for gentle lighting built into the benches caresses them.

In 1988, I made my first trip to the Viet Nam Memorial. Although I am not a veteran, the striking beauty of the monument and the silence moved me as people walked amongst so many names. I think American law enforcement now has such a hallowed place.

I was at the monument on October 14th, and was amazed by the many different ways people dealt with their missing loved ones. Many left flowers, especially single red roses, at the section with their loved one's name. Fellow officers taped patches or cards near a fallen comrade's name. One family left a cross of flowers with a photocopy of a newspaper article, whose headline read, "Killer Convicted". There were also crayon drawings from children to mommies and daddies, who no longer come home from work.

I was moved by the reactions of the people I saw that day. One was a very dignified, older gentleman, who had picked a Black Eyed Susan and found a piece of tape and taped the flower next to his son's name. He lost his son sixteen years ago, but, two thousand miles from home, he was able to find his son in good company amongst America's fallen heroes. He stood so proud, as tears flowed, while he honored his son.

Another person who also is a survivor was there. She lost her husband almost ten years prior. She has been so helpful to other survivors, and has done so much to see that this memorial was completed. She was walking with her daughter, and as she walked towards me, she had a big smile on her face. As our eyes met, I called her name, and she ran to me, gave me a hug and started to cry. They were tears of joy. She cried as she said, "It's finally here! We've all worked so long and so hard, and it's finally here!" Tears, hugs and tissues were the order of the day.

As I walked along with my friend, we saw another couple at the wall. They were an older couple, probably in their sixties. I thought the woman was crying so I offered her a tissue. She smiled and declined, saying it was just a cold. The man was doing an etching of a name on the wall. My friend asked whose name they were etching. I assumed it was their child's name. I was surprised when the man looked up, with a smile on his face, and said, "It's our father. He was killed many years ago. He was an officer in a little town and we thought they never reported his death. We're so happy to find his name with the others." Finding his name brought out feelings of joy. They now knew their father was with other heroes where he belonged. Hours later, still beaming, the man told my wife, Lynn, how thrilled he was and how much it meant to see his father's name.

On the afternoon of October 14th, survivors started to read the names of all 12,561 fallen heroes. This continued by state for over twenty-four hours, beginning with Alabama and ending with Federal officers. Everyone who read, no matter what time of the day or night, considered it an honor to be selected for such an important task.

Besides the survivors, there were other special people there. I met two gentlemen from Detroit —Marv who is a retired police officer and his friend Terry, who is still working as a police officer. They originally came to see the monument and meet other officers. Shortly after they arrived, they started to meet the survivors, and suddenly, they found the true purpose of their trip, to be with the survivors and share the experience with them. To show what special people they are — and they are only two of many of these special people--they were told by some friends they had made at the hotel, that a father was alone and his son's name would be read with the other officers from his state at 1:30 in the morning. The friends told them about this survivor, were from a different state. However, they put on their uniforms, went with this father and formed a special honor guard. Marv and Terry stood on either side of the fallen officer's father. As each name from his home state was called, this proud survivor stood, and saluted as each name was announced. These people add dignity and respect to this memorial.

On October 15th, a warm sunny day, President George H. W. Bush and Mrs. Barbara Bush joined the memorial committee and survivors, and the National Law Enforcement Memorial was dedicated. It was a gift from a caring America. Donations came not only from the Fraternal Order of Police, Police Benevolent Associations and other police organizations, but also from businesses and most importantly from the American people. Some donations were from ordinary people who care, and others came from special people, like the two young daughters of a fallen police officer, who sold their extra toys at a garage sale and donated the money to be sure that their daddy's name would be on the monument.

There seems to be a rebirth of patriotism in America. Our latest veterans have been embraced upon their return from wars in the Middle East. Maybe this same patriotism will someday include America's law enforcement community, who has been waging a war on crime and losing warriors for almost two hundred years.

Caring and giving is common amongst people at the monument. Police survivors always care, and always share. This monument provides them with the opportunity to share another moment with their loved one, and to say what needs to be said. The beauty of the monument is — it isn't lonely like a cemetery. The fallen hero's name is always in good company with so many other brave souls.

When you travel to Washington, please stop and see the monument in Judiciary Square. While you are there, take the time to share a moment with a survivor. You will be happy you did.

TAKEOVER

By

Dennis N. Griffin

Sometimes people find themselves in situations that require them to place themselves in harm's way in order to assist their fellow man. Las Vegas, Nevada, newsman Robert Stoldal found himself in that situation in August 1979. When asked, he answered the call.

At approximately nine o'clock on the morning of Saturday, August 25, 1979, inmates took control of the Clark County, Nevada, Jail Annex, located on the second floor of the Las Vegas City Hall complex on Stewart Avenue. This would be the longest siege ever handled by the Las Vegas Metropolitan Police Department. It was an incident that had all the ingredients of a Hollywood action movie: hardcore cons facing long sentences with little to lose; security equipment not working; procedures not followed and escape within the grasp of the inmates, although they didn't know it. A future sheriff, Jerry Keller, a sergeant at the time, was the primary negotiator for the police side.

At that time, the Annex was used primarily to house sentenced prisoners—mostly felons awaiting transfer to the state prison system in Carson City. On this particular day, eighty-four inmates were assigned to the facility. Among them were Patrick McKenna, Felix Lorenzo, and Eugene Shaw. McKenna and Lorenzo had recently been transferred to the Annex after having been implicated in a plot to start a riot at the Clark County Detention Center.

McKenna was a thirty-three-year-old white male with a long history of problems with the law. An escape artist and convicted rapist, he was serving three life sentences plus seventy-five years for sexually assaulting two women in Las Vegas in 1978. He was also facing a murder charge for killing his cellmate while housed in the Clark County Detention Center.

Lorenzo, a Latino, was thirty-years-old at the time. He'd been sentenced to 160 years in prison for numerous armed robberies. He'd taken hostages during his crimes capers, and on one occasion held an off-duty Metro officer captive for a short period of time. He was no stranger to prison strife, having been incarcerated at the Attica Correctional Facility in New York State during the infamous riot in 1971.

Shaw, a forty-one-year-old black male, was another convicted armed robber, doing a sixty year sentence.

What these convicts did that morning was no spur of the moment act. On the contrary, it was a well-planned escape attempt devised after a careful study of guard activities and jail procedures. The plot included paying an inmate trustee to leave a security gate ajar that led to the gun lockers where correction officers stored their service weapons. The warning light that would have alerted the guard in the Control Booth of the open door had been out of service for some time due to a mechanical malfunction. Whether this was known by the prisoners or a matter of pure luck is unclear.

In addition to these three prisoners, the three correction officers on duty that day would play major roles in the incident as hostages. David Murray, age thirty-five, Robert Hansen, fifty-two, and William Melton, also fifty-two, were all veteran officers with many years of experience.

At a few minutes after nine that morning, Eugene Shaw completed mopping the floor of the cellblock in which he, Lorenzo, and McKenna were housed. Officer Hansen was observing Shaw through the glass panel of the cellblock's locked security door. The officer later said that he'd never seen any of the inmates in that particular block work so hard.

Another door allowing access to the hallway outside the cellblock door was unlocked and open. Although contrary to policy and procedure, this door was apparently routinely left unsecured.

Inmate Shaw advised Hansen that he had finished his work and the cleaning materials could be removed from the cellblock. He pushed the nearly full mop pail toward the security door.

Hansen opened the door without first locking the inmates in their cells. He then bent over to grab the heavy bucket and lift it over the raised threshold. As he did, Shaw said, "Here, that's heavy; let me give you a hand."

Using this ruse, Shaw approached the stooped-over guard and struck him on the back of the neck. Before he fell, Hansen was able to reach up and activate an alarm button in a control panel next to the door.

Inmate Lorenzo, who had been in the cellblock's day room, joined Shaw and finished overpowering Hansen. They beat the officer until he was nearly unconscious. Correction Officer Murray, responding to the alarm, was also taken hostage.

Lorenzo removed the key to the gun locker from Hansen's pocket and exited the cellblock. Crouching low to avoid detection by the security cameras, he arrived at the gun-locker gate, which the trustee accomplice had left open. In a few seconds, he had possession of Hansen's 9 mm semi-automatic pistol. After arming himself, Lorenzo located the remaining guard, William Melton, in the booking area and took him prisoner at gunpoint. The Annex was now entirely in the control of the criminals.

Joined by McKenna, the three inmates stripped the guards, donned their uniforms and were ready for their escape. Unfortunately for them, they didn't realize that the elevator located next to the gun lockers and controlled from the main

Control Booth would have taken them to the first floor and freedom. Instead, they attempted to exit the front jail entrance, but were blocked by detectives who had responded to the alarm activated by Officer Hansen. The inmates retreated back into the interior of the jail where the captured guards had been left handcuffed. The escape attempt was aborted and the incident turned into a hostage situation.

After letting a few selected inmates whom they trusted out of their cells, the three ringleaders returned to the gun lockers. They retrieved the service weapons of Officers Murray and Melton, along with a .380 semi-automatic pistol. This gave the bad guys an arsenal of four handguns, three loaded 9 mm magazines, and a box of ammunition for the .380.

As they searched through the facility, they came across something almost as valuable to them as the weapons: a complete department Policy & Procedure Manual. While watching for police activity on the TV monitors covering the entrances, the convicts could now read about how the cops planned to respond to various jail incidents, how SWAT units would be deployed, and the techniques that might be used by Metro negotiators.

Outside the jail, uniformed personnel quickly contained the exterior of the building; two six-man SWAT teams were put into position in the corridor outside the jail entrance and elsewhere in the immediate area.

The recently created Hostage Negotiation Team made contact with the inmates via the cellblock phone system. Felix Lorenzo identified himself as the spokesman for the convicts; Patrick McKenna was later identified as the "security chief." For the next several hours, Lorenzo refused to discuss a resolution to the standoff directly with the police. Instead, he insisted on face-to-face meetings with specific local newsmen and attorneys whom he felt could be trusted more than the lawmen. The situation remained deadlocked until the police agreed to arrange for the requested third-party mediators.

Each side had concerns about the other that needed to be resolved before meetings could begin. The cops were afraid that the mediator could be a tempting target for the inmates to add to their cache of hostages. The inmates worried about a forced entry by a SWAT team and that their negotiator might get picked off or captured during the negotiating sessions.

To discourage a police assault, the felons periodically moved their hostages around, handcuffing them in close proximity to various points of entry.

The safety of the negotiators was addressed in a mutual agreement. A table was placed half in and half out of the jail-entrance door. This allowed the inmate negotiator—either Lorenzo or McKenna—to sit at the enclosed end of the table with limited exposure. The civilian mediator would remain in the open and be less apt to be harmed or taken prisoner by the convicts.

For further protection of the mediator, the police assigned a marksman to a position in a nearby parking structure whenever meetings were in progress. Overlooking the negotiating table at a distance of about twenty-five yards, the sniper was under instructions to shoot if it appeared the third party was in danger of being harmed or taken prisoner. As an additional precaution, several SWAT members were concealed in a stairwell close to the meeting site, ready to respond quickly to any threatening behavior by the inmates. A member of the Hostage Negotiation Team, too, was out of sight, but within earshot of the sessions.

Eighteen hours after taking control of the Annex, the inmates released a list consisting of ten demands to Deputy Public Defender Tom Leen, one of the mediators approved by the convicts. They related to such things as the availability of a law library and medical services, improved visitation, phone calls, and food.

Most of these concerns had previously been brought to the attention of jail authorities through the appropriate channels and found to have some merit. Changes were in fact being developed at the time of the takeover.

While the police were preparing responses to the initial demands, they maintained phone contact with Lorenzo and McKenna. Just prior to noon on Sunday, McKenna asked for newspapers, inmate mail and medication.

At this point a second mediator was brought aboard. He was Bob Stoldal, News Director of KLAS-TV.

Thirty-two years later, Bob Stoldal still has vivid memories of his participation in the jail incident. He remembers that he was recruited as a mediator directly by Patrick McKenna.

"I was at the TV station when the phone rang; it was Patrick. He identified himself and the situation. I'd never met him before, but I knew his father. He said he knew who I was and that he wanted a member of the media to act as an intermediary between the inmates and the police. We discussed the issue and I agreed to come down to the jail, which I did," the reporter says.

Stoldal's involvement was acceptable to Metro. He had a good relationship with them, having covered the cop beat for several years. They knew him personally, and his mother had worked in the records section of the former Las Vegas Police Department.

By accepting McKenna's offer, the reporter placed himself in a very dangerous situation. His role would place him face to face with armed convicts with little or no concern for his well-being. They could kill him or attempt to take him hostage at their whim. And if the bad guys did make a move on him, he could very well become a victim of friendly fire by the law enforcement personnel assigned to protect him. In spite of these risks, Stoldal entered the arena.

"The table where I met with the inmates was positioned so that they would be sitting inside the room and couldn't get to me very easily. I stayed outside the room, leaving them about ten or twelve feet away from me and behind a high counter. That arrangement gave both of us some protection," Stoldal recalls.

"I would take food up to the inmates and bring messages back to the officers, more of a messenger than a negotiator," he continued. "I remember the first time I went up there alone to meet McKenna. I kept looking at him and asked if he was pointing a gun at me; he said he wasn't. Since I didn't see any upside to him shooting me, I tended to believe him. I don't know how many trips I made up those stairs, but I'll tell you that the walk up always seemed longer than the walk back."

At one point, Metro wanted the inmates to show the newsman the hostages to verify their condition. "An image sticks in my mind of one of the guards being brought out behind the counter. I asked him how he was and he said he was okay. I remember he looked very scared and a little beat up," Stoldal recalled.

"I don't know as saying I felt threatened or afraid would be the right words," he explained. "You kind of get in a zone during something like that. I do remember that I always looked directly at the inmates so as not to show any fear and to be as calm as possible, as conversational as possible. About the middle of the second day, one of the members of the police negotiating team pulled me aside and kind of shook me. 'You've got to be more careful,' he warned me. He was concerned that I might be getting too friendly with the inmates. He wanted to remind me that these were the 'bad guys' and not to trust them. 'It's a matter of life or death,' he said."

Stoldal was aware of the sniper positioned in the parking garage and that he would be in the direct line of fire should the inmates make a move on him. He was under orders that if he felt threatened; he was to dive to his right behind a large metal trash container and crawl away. Thankfully, that never became necessary.

Years later, Stoldal joked with Jerry Keller, "Which way was I supposed to dive? I never could remember."

As these meetings continued and the police pressed for the release of the captured guards, unbeknownst to Stoldal or the cops, things were deteriorating inside the jail. Although the inmates had allowed each of the hostages to telephone his family—viewed as a positive development— two of the ringleaders were in sharp disagreement over what to do next.

Felix Lorenzo reportedly wanted to kill Officer Murray over a previous altercation. Eugene Shaw was allegedly concerned about what Lorenzo and McKenna might do, and wanted to contain them so that he could surrender to the police.

At approximately five-thirty Monday morning, nearly 48 hours into the escape attempt, Sgt. Keller was on the phone with McKenna. The inmate was seated on the floor outside the door to the on-duty Sergeant's Office. Officer Melton was handcuffed to a chair nearby. In a major breakthrough, Keller convinced McKenna to release Melton as a sign of good faith.

Just as Keller was cradling the handset, he heard the sound of gunshots over the phone and immediately called back. An inmate named Kuzman answered the phone. He advised Sgt. Keller that there had been a gunfight and that Shaw and Lorenzo were dead.

Kuzman was ordered to unload all weapons and surrender, an order with which he complied. McKenna stripped off the correction officer's uniform he was wearing and walked out of the jail with Officers Hansen and Murray to surrender. Officer Melton, who had sustained a minor hand wound during the shootout, remained inside. SWAT personnel cleared the facility and all of the inmates were subsequently transferred to the Clark County Detention Center.

In the investigation that followed, physical evidence and interviews with personnel and inmates were used to reconstruct the final moments of the siege.

It was determined that while McKenna was negotiating by phone with Sgt. Keller, Shaw and Lorenzo became engaged in a violent argument in a corridor a few feet from McKenna's location. Shooting erupted between the two, switching from position to position during the gunfight. Eventually, Lorenzo fell dead inside the Sergeant's Office, but not before wounding Shaw. During the gunfire, Officer Melton suffered a bullet wound to his left hand.

With Lorenzo disposed of, Shaw turned his attention to McKenna, who was still inside the Sergeant's Office. The inmates exchanged fire; McKenna's aim was more accurate. Within a few seconds, Shaw joined Lorenzo as an ex-inmate.

Patrick McKenna was charged in Shaw's death, but was acquitted. He did, however, receive an additional ninety-two year sentence for his role in the takeover. In 1980 he was convicted of murdering his cellmate while in the Clark County Detention Center.

Bob Stoldal continued his career as one of the most respected newsmen in Las Vegas. On June 30, 2008, he retired from KLAS-TV after thirty-six years there. He unretired a year later to become executive vice president of news at KVBC-TV in Las Vegas.

THE YOUNGEST HERO:

Death of an Innocent

By

Robert Fregeau

While doing research for a story to contribute to this anthology, I encountered a brief mention in Wikipedia regarding a young U.S. Marine from the Vietnam War. As I read the article, I could feel a bond beginning to form due to the manner in which we entered military service.

I entered the U.S. Air Force in 1954, just two days after my seventeenth birthday. My reasons for enrolling at such a young, tender age were varied and personal, but suffice it to say "I needed to grow up." I thought military service was the place to find maturity. But this story isn't about me; it's about a young Marine who should have never been where he was when he died.

The first similarity in this nexus of events is that Dan Bullock and this writer both emanated from broken homes. This can have a traumatic effect on a child; both positive and negative. By that I mean the child can both retreat into himself and milk the effects of the breakup of the family or he/she can get on with life and make the best of it. It appears we both took the positive road.

At the age of thirteen while residing in North Carolina with his mother and sister, Dan Bullock's mother passed away. Both he and his younger sister Gloria were relocated to Brooklyn, New York where they resided with their biological father and step-mother. This author was unable to ascertain Dan Bullock's circumstances during this period, but records show he had dreams of entering the military to become a pilot, a police officer or a U.S. Marine. His latter dream was realized.

Whether he garnered some assistance or completed the task in stealth mode, Dan Bullock, at the age of fourteen, managed to transform the date of birth on his birth certificate, to reflect an age of eighteen years. On September 18, 1968 he was officially sworn in as a United States Marine.

Somehow, he withstood the rigors of boot camp at Parris Island, South Carolina. This author has personal knowledge that men twice his age have had issues completing basic training in the Marine Corps. Within six months of completing basic training, Dan Bullock had *boots on the ground* with the 2nd Battalion, 5th Marines at An Hoa Combat Base in Vietnam.

On the night of June 7, 1969 the North Vietnamese Army attacked the base at An Hoa. It has been noted that members of his squad were running low on ammunition. Private First Class Dan Bullock made two runs to resupply the squad with ammo. It was on his second trip that he was killed by hostile small arms fire at the age of fifteen.

This author has a question that will forever remain unanswered. Were PFC Bullock's remains returned to U.S. soil on commercial aircraft as unaccompanied baggage? If true, this is an unforgivable act.

Now that we know the story of this heroic young man, the inferences of mishandling his remains will remain silent to honor his memory. As we approach another Memorial Day, one fact stands out very clearly… At the tender age of fifteen, PFC Dan Bullock went on record as the youngest United States Marine to die in the Vietnam War.

WHAT WAS YOUR NAME DOC?

By

Charles McKee

I never saw Doctor Good Guy when he was not smiling, and without a moment for a joke or a good word. He treated everyone as if they were the most important person with him at that specific moment. Patients, families, nurses, law enforcement officers or emergency personnel, it didn't seem to matter to him.

Brookside hospital was a hot bed of activity for all workers during the weekend as it provided medical services for three surrounding cities, and a very large unincorporated area. It was a hospital that saw DOA victims of shooting, stabbings, and the like every day, especially on Friday and Saturday nights.

Dr. Unknown was always in the middle of the surge in emergency medical activities at this busy suburban Hospital. He had the ability to motivate co-workers and staff to accomplish anything that needed to be done in and around the hospital setting. He had a special talent of speaking with victims and staff as if he had hours that could be spent talking at that exact moment.

Most women would say he was a handsome fellow, and young men marveled at the fact that he loved and drove his Porsche every chance he got. To say that this man, this doctor, had respect from the community is without question.

This Doc spent many extra minutes explaining medical procedures to me as I developed my deep interest in emergency medicine. We often spent a few moments over a cup of coffee in between the flood tide of emergencies that were always present at Brookside Hospital.

Having spent many hours with this man, I saw a real man who possessed not only a medical background, but, a background in humanity that reached everyone he came into contact with.

The west end of Contra Costa County and the staff of Brookside were heartbroken to see the Doc leave to enter his own practice in the east end of the county. We were also shocked to find that he had opened his practice right in the middle of a very high crime rated area. The locations boasted some of the poorest members of Contra Costa County. This man was always in the middle of helping people.

While on patrol, I would drive by his office late in the evening, to find that he was still seeing patients. This man was busy, and we all garnered a deep respect for him in every sense of the word. One evening as we sat through patrol lineup; the duty sergeant reported that the Doc had driven his beloved Porsche into an abutment early that morning, killing him instantly.

A community hero was gone; like the flicker of a dying candle. And, I anguish now over the fact that I cannot remember his name. Maybe Doctor Hero, leader and friend will do for now.

WHERE IS OUR PATRIOTISM?

By

Keith Bettinger

April 16, 2011, Lynn and I went to see the military tattoo at the Thomas and Mack Center here in Las Vegas, NV. The doors opened at 6:30 p.m. and I wanted to be there when it opened because I expected a large crowd and a huge traffic jam on Tropicana Avenue leading into the arena.

When Lynn and I arrived, we breezed into the parking lot. We parked near the entrance. There was no need to display the handicapped parking permit for these two fledgling senior citizens. Inside the arena were tables and booths set up to recruit musicians for local bands, selling items and asking for support for wounded warriors or military families in need.

When Lynn and I took our seats about one-half hour before show time, the arena was near empty. Here we were at the top of the seating section looking down into acres of empty seats. As the clock ticked away to three minutes until show time, people took some of the empty seats, but only in a trickle, no mass arrival.

Military bands from the United States, Great Britain and Canada along with police pipe bands from Vancouver and Winnipeg Police Departments, as well as the 3rd Infantry Division "Old Guard" silent drill team, marched en masse into the arena and rendered honors to special guests. The shame of it all is when I looked around, I thought there were more people on the arena floor than there were in the seats.

Later on that evening, as Lynn and I came out of the casino where we had dinner, a bus was dropping off the United States Marine Corps band from 29 Palms. Lynn was almost in tears as she said, "They're so young."

Yes dear they are young, and they're all volunteers. They are giving their youth so we can remain safe as we grow old and comfortable. They are some of the most under-appreciated heroes you will ever meet. Yet they go into harms-way willingly and without question.

This leads me to my questions; *"where is our patriotism? When did it leave us behind? What happened to honoring our heroes, decorating graves on Memorial Day, attending Memorial Day parades, and most importantly honoring all they have done by standing and rendering honors as our Nation's flag goes by?"* Maybe the most important question of the evening during the tattoo was, why was the arena empty?

Las Vegas is a military town. We are home to Nellis Air Force Base. The United States Air Force Thunderbirds call Las Vegas home. When University of Nevada at Las Vegas has a basketball game at the Thomas and Mack Center, there are lines of cars waiting to enter the parking field while blocking lanes of traffic on Tropicana Avenue. On the evening news after a game, sportscasters interview players and some of them can't even string a coherent sentence together, yet Americans flood the arena to see them run up and down a basketball court.

There is something wrong in this country when we fail to honor our true heroes. The audience made up for the empty seats with rousing standing ovations, but as a town we could have done more to welcome and support our heroes. They are willing to give all to protect us. The least we can do is thank them and show our appreciation.

BOB HOPE – PATRIOT

By

Rena C. Winters

It seemed that he had always been there like a part of our family. First it was his radio shows, next his motion pictures and then television where he came into every home in the USA. He was known as America's greatest showman and that's true. However, he could also be called America's greatest patriot because of the millions of lives he touched through his endless USO tours where he entertained, bringing hope, joy and laughter to American combat troops at the front lines and in the hospitals. His devotion to his country and the men and women who served in the armed forces was unlimited.

Bob mastered every comic venue, vaudeville, Broadway, radio, movies and television and over his career collected hundreds of humanitarian awards. However his greatest accomplishment was his unfailing response to the USO and providing entertainment for our military forces on all its battlefields and in all its wars for over a half century.

The troops loved him and so did the families of the military men and women back home. Although a member of the mostly jaded entertainment industry, I would always feel the chills go up and down my spine when I would see Bob and his current troupe at some front line military outpost or hear him sing "Thanks For The Memory." Then, out of the blue, my job put me in contact with Bob and the USO.

In 1980 I was writer and associate producer of the ninety minute special "My Little Corner Of The World." This show was designed with a heavy dose of 'Americana' that included long segments devoted to the United States Military Academy at West Point. These included the West Point Corps of Cadets in a special dress parade in honor of General William C. Westmoreland who was also interviewed. An outstanding performance by the famous West Point Glee Club and a review of the football eras of Glenn Davis , Felix "Doc" Blanchard and Peter Dawkins, all of them Heisman Trophy winners.

Other segments include the advent of jazz and gospel, truly America's gift to the world of music coming up the Mississippi from New Orleans then spreading throughout the land.

The smashing climax, that won vast critical acclaim, was shot during a rain storm at historic Valley Forge, the Nation's Shrine, with the historic Medal of Honor Grove serving as the background.

However, something vital was missing. It was Bob Hope and his famous USO military tours. I picked up the phone and called Bob's headquarters in Tolucca Lake, California hoping to speak to one of his assistants. The minute I mention the USO Bob was the line asking what he could do for me.

I told him that the show was about America and I didn't want to do the show without spotlighting him and his work with the USO. With his heavy schedule it was impossible for him to join our cast and crew at West Point but he would be happy to package film clips from his visits to troops in Vietnam including a heartwarming Christmas Eve performance with Les Brown and his Orchestra plus the famous stars that went on that trip. As a major plus he would go into the studio and film a special salute to our show and the USO. I held my breath when I asked what his fee would be, then I heard that famous Bob Hope laugh. "Honey we're not going to talk about fees. This is for the USO and America."

As promised, the clips and his special salute arrived a few days later. He was celebrating his silver anniversary with the USO. Twenty-five years of performances around the world.

When we edited our show, Bob's clips and USO salute fit perfectly. The American public responded to the program and was awarded the Freedoms Foundation and American Family Heritage awards.

I returned the film to Bob at his headquarters before the show was released to thank him for his help. He was the same man I had watched since childhood. Warm and funny taking time to thank us for having him when it was really the other way around.

Bob Hope, a man for all seasons left us when he was 100.

I miss him. His talent, his warmth and his eternal giving of himself to the USO and America's military. I don't think there will ever be another like him. Greatest entertainer and a super patriot who proved over and over again how much he loved this wonderful country.

Our country, yours and mine, our little corner of the world.

PAID IN FULL

By:

Keith J. Bettinger

I am sitting at my desk, but what I should be doing is cleaning the house. Since we need to paint the room, and we are thinking of moving eventually, I have packed away almost all my police memorabilia. This includes all but one of my law enforcement uniform patches, Right now, there are over one thousand patches in a box waiting to be mounted or placed in an album, so they can be displayed. However, there is one patch, in a frame, all by itself. It sits on my desk, because it is special to me.

The patch is not a fancy emblem. It is just black and gold. All it has on it is the name of the community, the word "POLICE" and a gold star embroidered at the bottom. It is not a new patch. In fact, it is rather battered and worn. It is not the type of patch over which most collectors would make a fuss. You might be wondering what is so special about this patch? I will tell you why it is special, — it has a history and a story all its own.

In January 1991, I was assigned to work investigations in my precinct's plainclothes unit. One afternoon, I was sitting at my desk, shuffling through my cases. The telephone rang. It was a police officer, from the Midwest, calling to speak specifically to me. He had read one of my articles about living through the effects of post shooting trauma. He said he enjoyed it and it was informative. Now he needed more information.

His brother, also a police officer, had been in a shooting. The officer was not only concerned about his brother's personal safety, but also his physical and emotional well being. He asked if I had any more information on post shooting trauma. He wanted to know more about what to do for his brother. He also wanted to know if I would speak to his brother, if he needed to talk to someone.

I told him that I had written a few more articles on post shooting trauma, and I would be more than happy to send him copies. We discussed the symptoms of post shooting trauma. What to look for and what to do to help his brother, if any problems arose. I told him I would be more than happy to speak to his brother, and was available anytime his brother needed me. I also told him I had a friend who was a police officer and a peer support person. This friend lived only a couple miles from the officer and his brother. This friend would be someone nearby if they needed immediate help.

The officer thanked me and wanted to know what he could do to repay me. I told him I appreciated his thinking so highly of my work, and that was enough. I did add that I was a patch collector, and said if he could send me a couple patches, from his area, it would be appreciated.

Awhile later, I heard from the officer. His brother was working his way through the shooting aftermath and the struggles that came with it. He thanked me for my help and told me he would keep me informed of his brother's progress. He also said he was working on obtaining some patches for my collection. That was the last I heard from him.

One day, a few years later; I was using my computer. I was on one of the on-line services. Lo and behold, while in one of the law enforcement areas, I found the name and e-mail address of the officer who contacted me. I sent a quick note. I asked how his brother was, and included a little dig, "By the way where are those patches?" I received an e-mail note telling me his brother was doing well and the patches would be coming soon.

A few days later a large envelope arrived. I opened it, and found it was full of patches. Inside were patches from his department, his former department, and patches from neighboring departments. There also was a patch from the department his brother had transferred to since the shooting. His brother had become a high ranking supervisor in the new department. The last patch I took out was the old beaten up one. It had a note on it. The note said, "I know this doesn't look like much, but this patch was on the uniform my brother was wearing the day of his shooting. When he left the department he kept that shirt. He took one patch off and kept it for himself.

I took the other one for you. It belongs to you. Without your help I don't know if my brother would be here today. Your help made a difference. If there is anything I can do for you, give me a call. If you want some other patches, just let me know."

I sat down and wrote a note. I wanted to let the officer know, he did not owe me a thing. I was paid in full.

WHAT WAS IT LIKE WHEN...

by

Keith Bettinger

I enjoy studying history. I watch the History Channel, read the tomes of Stephen Ambrose, and read historical novels. I am a baby boomer, a member of the generation that came to be when our heroes returned from World War II.

When I read about the attack on Pearl Harbor, I wonder what went through the minds of the American public as they heard the news that the American military had been attacked. I wondered what it was like to suddenly be pulled into a war. My mother can still tell me stories about rationing, food and gas coupons, and friends going off to war. Every community has a memorial to those friends and heroes who did not return.

The war of my generation, the Viet Nam War, was a long and protracted war. It too has many heroes that are now growing gray. It was not like World War II. It had been around for years, and slowly swallowed up the youth of the United

States. Our returning veterans were not treated with the respect they deserved. The Viet Nam war did not answer the question for our generation, what was it like when Pearl Harbor was attacked?

Now we have our answer. On September 11, 2001, terrorists stole our aging innocence. On that day, America was plunged into a new war; probably different from any other it has ever fought. This time our military was not the only target. Symbols of American pride were destroyed. Along with the twin towers went thousands of civilians working in many different occupations, while they tried to secure the American dream. Stolen from us along with all those civilians are the heroes of the New York City Fire Department, the New York City Police Department, the Port Authority Police Department, and the military and civilian personnel at the Pentagon, who went into the burning buildings to rescue people while others were fleeing for their lives.

In the history of law enforcement and fire fighting, losses of these staggering proportions have never been seen before. The losses from this horrific event took more lives than those lost during the attack on Pearl Harbor.

Baby boomers, who wanted to know what it was like when Pearl Harbor was attacked and America was plunged into war, now have their answer. The "other" generation can tell you where they were on December 7, 1941. Many generations can tell you where they were when they received the news that President John F. Kennedy was killed, and now we all will remember where we were on September 11, 2001. We now know what it was like when the United States was attacked and plunged into war. It has happened to us. May God Bless America!

POWER OF THE AMERICAN PRESS (IMO)*

By

Jack Miller

During WWII I was in grade school. I recall seeing flags in the windows of homes indicating a family member, a son or daughter was serving in the military. The population was for our being involved. Newspapers and radio news reporters were in favor or our involvement. They wanted a resolution to the war and dedication to the effort that was there. To be anti-military then would have been unpatriotic.

Then came the Cold War, a continuing state of political and military tension between the United States, its NATO** allies and the Soviet Union and her satellite nations erupted, but few even noticed. The American press reported on the Berlin Airlift and how shameful it was that the Soviet Union would blockade Berlin and cause the suffering of the people. They might even talk about stopping communism in some parts of the world. But generally the American press was becoming ambivalent, and as a result so were the American people.

During the Korean conflict I was in high school. I recall newsmen and reporters talking and writing that we should not be involved in this conflict, however they still showed support. Soldiers were respected. Citizens generally did not display the Blue Star "service flag" in their windows. A soldier in uniform was treated to free coffee in many restaurants; free bus rides in their home towns. Our troops had held the communists at the thirty-eighth parallel in Korea and many came home. That was in 1952. What many people did not realize is that the Korean "Police Action" has not ended yet. Only a cease fire has been agreed to and that keeps the North Koreans above the thirty-eighth parallel, so it is still a war zone. However, you will not see that in any newspapers, on TV, or being reported on the radio. We still have troops there in support of our allies, the South Koreans.

I enlisted in the Army in 1955. I was proud to wear the uniform. The free coffee might be gone to the uniformed service member except at the USO, but in some towns like Detroit, servicemen in uniform still could ride the busses free. Very few displayed the service flags in windows. My folks did not. Thinking back I have to ask myself were they ashamed? No, a resounding no! It just wasn't thought of. The media rarely discussed the Cold War. That didn't sell commercials for their profit.

Along came Vietnam and it was the anti-war sentiment that became the news of the day. If more than five people got together and held signs protesting the war, it was reported in the media. If someone burned their draft card, there was a news camera covering the event. Service flags became a thing of the past. Even some politicians, the same ones who sent the troops to Vietnam came out against that conflict because the media made it popular to be anti-war and anti-military. Why, because the media reported that babies and children had been killed during that conflict. Who killed them was immaterial. A communist bullet or an American bullet, it was treated the same according to the media. Americans became responsible for all Vietnam deaths. With all this media attention, public opinion was swayed. A soldier in uniform was spit on by some, and called names by others, with "baby killer" being one of the more popular. Service members serving within the United States or returning from overseas were advised not to wear their uniforms off stations, bases and posts, or while travelling so as to avoid these situations.

There were other minor skirmishes, like Grenada, involving American troops with little or no reporting and certainly no reporting for any length of time. If you recall as I do, there was little commitment to the cause whether just or unjust.

So when 9-11 occurred, I was in a state of shock when the media all came out for going to war to avenge the surprise attack on New York and Pennsylvania. The enemy lost fourteen that day and we lost 3,000. The media reported and reported and reported more. For thirty days they repeated their reports showing the collapsing of the towers. The power of the American press cited the passion of the American people and again the people displayed their American flags and the small service flags announcing to everyone who looked that they proudly had a relative in the military in service of their country.

As of this writing it has been almost twelve years since we were attacked. This is the longest hot war we have had.

My advice to the reader is to be careful. The media is starting to send its reporters out to cover the peace marchers, the flag burners and the anti-war effort which are always present. Try to remain supportive of the military personnel who have volunteered to serve. Display your service flags. Display your American Flag. Keep pressure on the media to support the War on Terrorism for as long as it takes. Remember, the United States is our country. It should not be controlled by the attitudes of the media.

*In My Opinion

** North Atlantic Treaty Organizations

THE DAY THE OLD DETECTIVE CRIED

By:

Keith Bettinger

In February and March of 2002 I was doing a lot of traveling. I went to Anchorage, Alaska with a friend to do a presentation for law enforcement trainers. Alaska in winter is beautiful. From there I went to Southern California to visit a friend and his family. The high desert is also magnificent. After California I drove to Las Vegas to visit my son who lives there and to put a down payment on my new family home.

While visiting Las Vegas, I looked up an old friend, a retired detective from the police department we both retired from. Whenever I go to Las Vegas, I try to get together with this gentleman. He is the old time cop that movies are made about and from whence folklore is born. He has unique people skills and always got the police job done. To this day, he is still a legend in the department. In fact, he is the only detective I know of, who during his career, was returned to uniform for having a "discussion" with a less than astute supervisor, and later was returned to detective duties. He is also the father figure you can always call on when you need help. When a kid, far away from home, needs a Dutch uncle to help, this man is there with just one phone call. When he is told, "I owe you big time!" His response always is, "We're family. We're here for one another."

In March of 2002 while I was in Las Vegas, we got together. We met for lunch. After our greetings and then some small talk, the discussion turned to old friends and how they were. Later, the discussion, like all discussions between New Yorkers and former New Yorkers, turned to the attack of September 11, 2001.

He told me how after he retired, one of his jobs was driving a limousine. He made many trips into the World Trade Center with clients. In fact he made so many trips he became friends with the parking attendants in the underground garage. He bought them coffee on his frequent visits and chatted with them while waiting for his passengers.

This retired detective is the type of person who can make friends with anyone. He wondered out loud how well these people fared in the attack. He told me about some of his other friends. These were friends who did not make it out.

Always the cop's cop, the old detective is a member of the Blue Knights Motorcycle Club. He made many cross country motorcycle trips with his law enforcement friends. He also would make trips from Long Island into New York City on his motorcycle to visit police friends at their commands.

One of his friends was Mike Curtin, a New York City Police sergeant assigned to Emergency Services. Mike was a former sergeant major in the United States Marine Corps. He served in the Persian Gulf War and had a chest full of medals for heroism. Although he was as tough as steel, he had a heart that was as soft as butter. Mike was one of the cops who went in the World Trade Center during the rescue operations and never made it out. His nickname was Iron Mike. According to my friend, Mike was invincible. He spoke reverently about Mike's family and how important they were to Mike. He went on to say what a great friend Mike was to all who knew him.

My friend's voice started to change, and the tears followed. This was something I had never seen or heard from this tough old time detective before. I gave him his time and space. He had to grieve once again. He had to work his way through his thoughts and memories.

After a while, he wiped his eyes, and we started to talk about the temporary memorial that was being set up at the World Trade Center site; towering twin blue lights. I told my friend I was hoping to view the towering lights on my flight home the next evening.

The next night the flight home was uneventful and even though I was happy to get home after three weeks of traveling, I was disappointed I didn't get to see the twin towers of light.

The next morning, my slumber was broken by a phone call from Suzie Sawyer of Concerns of Police Survivors. She needed a favor. Concerns of Police Survivors was doing a three day seminar on line of duty deaths near Buffalo, N.Y. The speaker for the third day was ill and unable to attend. She wanted to know if I would fill in. I put together my lecture material, made my airline reservations and got a ride to LaGuardia Airport.

At 6:30 that evening, I boarded my flight for Buffalo. As we left the airport, we flew over lower Manhattan. I looked out my window and there soaring into the heavens were the twin towers of blue light. Everyone on the plane moved to the left side of the plane and looked out the windows. Some sighed others commented on how beautiful the memorial looked, some of us were just silent.

As we left the area, I sat back in my seat and thought how I wished the old detective was with me on this flight, we could have shared a few tears together.

WHERE THERE'S HOPE

By

Ron Corbin

It was mid-December 1966. Anticipation and excitement with all the soldiers and airman was the topic of the day at the Army and Air Force bases at Pleiku, Republic of Vietnam. The Bob Hope/USO Christmas Show was scheduled to perform at Camp Holloway; a small Army helicopter base in the Central Highlands near the borders with Cambodia nd Laos.

Growing up, I had watched Bob Hope as a comedian on black and white television. For my dad, a World War II Navy veteran, I remember Bob Hope's name being spoken around our house of someone who brought laughter to the islands of the South Pacific. To me, he was a just a comedian who made me laugh when doing the "Road" movies with Bing Crosby and Dorothy Lamour.

But now, as an Army combat helicopter pilot, his appearance meant a lot more to me and the fact that I might have the chance to actually see him in person. Bob Hope symbolized a spirit of patriotic freedom; something we all believed in during the unpopular war in Asia. He countered the illusion back home of anti-war protesters, and that there were still some Americans who supported us.

Of course, in actuality as a twenty year-old male, I have to admit that my eagerness for the upcoming USO show was more likely the thrill of maybe getting to see some of the "hot" female stars who were possibly in his tour group; like Ann-Margret, Raquel Welch, and Joey Heatherton. Or maybe even, "These Boots Are Made For Walkin'" girl herself, Nancy Sinatra.

Bob Hope performed his first USO Show at California's March Field, on May 6, 1941; three months after the USO was formed. From the deserts of Africa to the Arctic tundra of Alaska and Greenland, from the frozen hills of Korea to the tropics of Vietnam, Bob and his USO entourage have traveled the World to reach out to U.S. troops. Bob and his show tours found no bounds of where they would provide a "Touch of Home" to America's GIs. His stage wasn't always formal, with performances being conducted wherever he could be seen by his audience. From the back of a truck on the "cow pasture circuit" in France in 1944-45 to aboard the Navy's most modern aircraft carriers. Since that first appearance in California, though, the name Bob Hope and the USO has become synonymous.

The United Service Organizations was a new organization, founded in response to a request from President

Franklin D. Roosevelt to provide morale and recreation services to U.S. uniformed military personnel. Roosevelt was elected as its honorary chairman. This request brought together six civilian organizations: the Salvation Army, Young Men's Christian Association (YMCA), Young Women's Christian Association (YWCA), National Catholic Community Service, National Travelers Aid Association and the National Jewish Welfare Board.

Sure over the years, there were many celebrities who accompanied Bob on these tours. From1941 to 1947, the USO presented more than 400,000 performances, featuring entertainers such as Bing Crosby, Jerry Colonna, Judy Garland, Bette Davis, Humphrey Bogart, Lauren Bacall, Frank Sinatra, Marlene Dietrich, Hattie McDaniel, Eubie Blake, Ann Sheridan, Laurel and Hardy, The Marx Brothers, Jack Benny, Larry Adler, Ossy Renardy, Zero Mostel, James Cagney, James Stewart, Gary Cooper, Doraine and Ellis, Lena Horne, Danny Kaye, The Rockettes, Al Jolson, Fred Astaire, Curly Joe DeRita, The Andrews Sisters, Joe E. Brown, Joe E. Lewis, Ray Bolger, Lucille Ball, Glenn Miller, Martha Raye, Mickey Rooney, Betty Hutton and Dinah Shore. But it was always "Bob Hope," who appeared or hosted nearly 200 of these shows, that generated the euphoria among the men and women serving in our military branches.

Bob Hope entertained until December 1990, when he brought laughter and Christmas cheer to troops participating in Operation Desert Shield in Saudi Arabia and Bahrain on his final USO tour. In 1997, the USO successfully worked with

Congress to designate Bob Hope the first honorary veteran of the U.S. armed forces. That same year, the "Spirit of Hope" Award debuted at the USO Gala. It is a portrait base-relief image of Bob Hope, created by St. Louis sculptor Don F. Wiegand and Michael Fagin, and is presented to distinguished Americans whose patriotism and service to the troops reflects that of Bob Hope.

Why would Bob devote most of his lifetime to this enterprise of "troop entertainment"? If there was any personal gain for Bob, it came not in the form of monetary enrichment. It had to be in his love for America, and for those who have sacrificed maintaining the freedoms we all enjoy.

"Back in 1941, at March Field, California...I still remember fondly that first soldier audience," Hope once said. "I looked at them, they laughed at me, and it was love at first sight."

What was it about Bob Hope that has made him an icon for nearly five generations; a personification reflecting this mission? Was it his humor and wit? Was it the movie stars and celebrities who he brought along to entertain? Was it gorgeous women that reminded the "American fighting man" just what they were fighting for? As a vet, I think it was all these things. In a nutshell, it gave the soldier, the sailor, the marine, and the airman something to not only build morale, but something much stronger. It gave them encouragement to continue in their endeavor. It gave them hope.

The USO's mission statement is, "USO lifts the spirits of America's troops and their families." And Bob, I can honestly say ... "Mission Accomplished."

I never got to see Bob Hope that Christmas season in 1966 Vietnam. I ended up having to sit in my helicopter with troops at the ready to be a reactionary security force for Bob and his tour group in case the VC or NVA decided to attack. Initially, I was a little disappointed, until I realized that Bob and his assemblage of talented performers were giving up their time with family back in the States to bring a little happiness to thousands of military personnel in a combat zone. Who was I to complain?

I came to the conclusion that, for the American military fighting troops ... past and present ... where there's Bob, there's "Hope."

THE SHRINE IN LAS VEGAS

By

Keith Bettinger

There's a touch of New York City in Las Vegas – old New York City – right at the corner of Las Vegas Boulevard and Tropicana Avenue. It's the New York - New York Casino. The facade has many of the stately old buildings that made up the neoclassical skyline of old New York. These buildings include the Empire State Building, Chrysler Building, New Yorker Hotel, the CBS Building, and the Seagram Building to name a few. The city front is one-third scale to the real buildings. There is also a harbor in front of the building containing not only a half million gallons of water, but the Brooklyn Bridge, the Statue of Liberty and two old-fashioned FDNY fireboats that spray water from their turret guns at regular intervals.

In the middle of the 1990s, on frequent trips to Las Vegas, I watched some of the construction of the New York - New York Casino. While watching the on-going construction, I thought it was strange there were no World Trade Center Towers. But as I watched the casino take shape, it was easy to see it was a representation of the old New York City buildings and monuments. Now it seems almost prophetic. Whether you look at the real Manhattan skyline or the one in Las Vegas, something is missing – two towers that were a part of the city and part of everyone in this country.

Something else is missing as well– almost 3,000 people. Of those lost twenty- three were New York City Police Officers, thirty-seven were Port Authority of New York and New Jersey Police Officers, and 343 were firefighters from the New York City Fire Department. They may be gone, but they are not forgotten. Immediately after September 11, 2001, an impromptu memorial at the New York – New York rose as if it was a *Phoenix* rising from the ashes. Right in front of the lagoon with the Statue of Liberty and the fireboats, items started to appear. As you walk past the site now, there are uniform shirts and tee shirts, patches and hats to commemorate not only the fallen heroes but all the heroes who gave a part of themselves in the rescue and recovery efforts.

As you start to walk from the north side of the lagoon, you begin to see and read the heartfelt reminders of not only that tragic day, but of the strength of the American people and the support of our friends from foreign countries, both near and far. There is a Chicago police department uniform shirt that has written across it, "Our hearts and prayers are with you always." Nearby is a simple bouquet of silk roses. Roses always symbolize a gift of love. The North Tonawanda, New York Police Department has a tee shirt placed on the fence. The entire department signed the shirt and each officer from the chief to the newest officer wrote their heartfelt sentiments to their comrades in New York City.

As you walk a little further south there is a tee shirt dedicated to the memory of the Vigiano brothers. Joseph Vigiano was a detective assigned to Emergency Service Squad Truck 2. He responded to the World Trade Center that day to do what members of Emergency Service do – rescue people. His brother John, a firefighter in company 132, did the same thing. In the plummeting rain of death and destruction, they were taken. Right near the Vigiano shirt there's a pair of inflatable American Flags with the inscription God Bless America

A child hung one of her shirts on the fence. It has a print of the Statue of Liberty on the front. Around the print of Lady Liberty is quite a magnificent tome about the horrors of September 11. But more importantly at the end, in large bold letters are the words of wisdom from a child who was robbed of innocence, "United we've fallen, United we'll rise. We will survive! Patricia DeRise 7/4/02". As I walked around looking at the tributes, a new one had been added by a couple of young police officers; it was a uniform shirt from Lake Zurich, Illinois. They took the time to neatly place the shirt without disturbing the many around and below it. They took a moment to reflect and touch the shirt one last time before moving on.

Other shirts nearby had some simple sentiments; "For Love of our fallen brothers." On a 'Firefighters for Christ' tee shirt was an inscription from the Bible, John 15:13, "Greater love has no one than this, that he lay down his life for his friends." The heroes of September 11 did that. Not all the heroes died that day, many worked tirelessly to find their fallen brothers and sisters in arms. They also spent their waking hours searching for the thousands of lost civilians they served.

Someone from Naperville, IL Police Department placed a tee shirt at the shrine. Besides having the patch on the shirt, an officer also placed a patch pin on the shirt. People stop to look. They touch it gently, even reverently, but no one will dare take it.

As I continued on my journey I saw a tee shirt from the Indianapolis, Indiana Fire Department. Two brothers who are firefighters placed the shirt, but their message was in memory of their uncle, Lieutenant General Timothy Maude, a victim of the attack on the

Pentagon. Sometimes we forget the other victims. Sometimes the tragedy is too large to remember in its entirety and we have to be reminded of it a piece at a time.

The Steelworkers of America cannot be forgotten. Not only did they put their hearts and souls into the construction of the World Trade Center, they were some of the first volunteers in to help with the search and recovery work. When their towers were destroyed, a part of them went with it. They have their union shirts mingled amongst those of the police, firefighters and emergency medical service personnel.

There are also foreign shirts on the fence. Some are from nearby, such as Calgary in Canada and some are from far away like the West Yorkshire Fire Service in Great Britain. They mingle amongst the shirts, hats and patches from across America.

Even though they pulled at my heart, I thought I was doing all right as I walked amongst these remembrances. Then I came to a worn and twisted pennant at the western end of the semicircular fence surrounding the lagoon. There was this blue banner with white letters that simply said, "New York Says Thank You America." My eyes misted and a lump was in my throat. Yes, New York does say thank you. Thank you for your help. Thank you for being there. Thank you for your contributions. Thank you for remembering and thank you for hurting and grieving with us.

It seems funny that in the middle of Las Vegas, a city known for never sleeping, there is a hushed silence as you walk amongst these memorial tributes. It is like walking into the Vietnam Memorial or the National Law Enforcement Officers Memorial. There is a sense that you are on hallowed ground and respect must be paid. Although many of these shirts have patches, they remain undisturbed. No one will take one; it would be a sacrilege to do so.

I started to worry, what will happen after September 11, 2002? Will the memorial be removed? Will it be business as usual once again? "Not a chance," I am happy to say. The New York – New York Casino not only held an unveiling of the hero stamp in front of the memorial on July 3, 2002, but they have just released their plan to install a permanent granite memorial to enshrine the mementoes. We will never forget the attack on our country and we will never forget the heroic sacrifice of our fallen heroes. Besides the memorials that will be dedicated at Ground Zero and the Pentagon, hopefully, there will always be a Shrine in Las Vegas.

WHAT IS A HERO

By

Marshal Taylor

I've been thinking about heroes lately, partly because the anthology our group is writing is about patriotism and heroes. I recognize that these are difficult times. We are fighting two wars, our tax laws are in serious need of updating to correct inequities and remove loopholes, and we owe a great deal of money to a country that is not our friend. Meanwhile, the real income of the middle class has dwindled in buying power, and we have people making laws for us, who don't seem to understand how our government works.

However, I guess I'm a glass-half-full kind of person. I have faith in the American people, and I think sooner or later, we will correct the problems we have now so that we can move on to newer ones. I know that we have slackers and graffiti taggers who seem to feel they owe nothing to society, but I also know that we have a core of young people who accomplish things and who will eventually become our leaders. I hear people moan about how today's youth are pampered and are not being serious, but I also know the same things were said by the ancient Greeks. Some things change, some things don't.

Anyway, I started out by talking about heroes, so I should end up on that subject. I think there are heroes walking amongst us every day, but that we don't recognize them because we think hero begins with a capital 'H'. The capital 'H' heroes are the ones who are decorated and recognized, like war heroes, or the first responders at the World Trade Center, and they are to be greatly admired. They give us inspiration and an ideal to measure ourselves by.

I also think there are small letter 'h' heroes, the ones who are never decorated and will never be recognized. I think the poorly paid worker who gets up every morning to go to a grinding job is a mundane hero. I think the ghetto kid who dreams about getting out and does something about it is a hero. To me, the single mom working two jobs to support her family is also heroic. I have seen a young man with a back so twisted that he limps, but he works as a box boy at a local grocery store, and I think he is heroic. I could go on and on with more examples, but let me sum it up by saying that I believe anyone who pushes against overwhelming odds and gets on with life is heroic. So, the next time you wonder where are today's heroes, instead of looking at our "leaders" or the "shakers and movers," and all the celebrities, maybe you can just look around you. I'll bet you can find heroes all over the place.

WHY WE ATTEND

By:

Keith Bettinger

During my career, I have attended many law enforcement funerals. They numbered more than I wanted to, and less than I should have attended. Many civilians question why so many officers attend another officer's funeral. They do not understand why officers go to pay their respects to someone they did not know. Most know it is to pay respect to a fallen hero. Some might be pessimistic and think it is just to attend a big party following the funeral. Others believe it is just to obtain a day off from work. There are probably many officers as well, who do not know why they have to be there. It is just that somewhere, deep down in their hearts, they know it is the proper thing to do.

Recently I was watching The History Channel on cable television. The program was about Arlington National Cemetery. The documentary took the time to visit and explain many of the special memorials and monuments within the hallowed grounds. The show gave a list of requirements needed to be met, in order to be buried in Arlington National Cemetery. It also told of the hierarchy of entitlements, as well as the significance, of the many rituals and ceremonies that are performed. Both the rider-less horse and the artillery caisson are reserved for military officers. The survivors of every buried veteran receive an American flag, folded in a triangle. This represents the tri-cornered hat of our patriotic Revolutionary War soldiers. It does not matter how big or small the funeral. Nor is it important whether the veteran's mortal remains are carried in a casket, or in an urn. Each deceased veteran receives a full honor guard; something to which he is entitled.

There was another special part of the ceremonies at Arlington National Cemetery explained by the show. It was shown in a rather sad but poignant way. There was a funeral. One man in a suit stood alone at a gravesite. There were four empty chairs behind him. The honor guard member presented him with the folded American Flag and thanked him on behalf of our country. From the corner of the television screen, came an officer escorting a woman. He presented her to the survivor. The woman was one of the "Arlington Ladies'". An Arlington Lady attends every funeral at Arlington National Cemetery. They pay their respects to the bereaved, and give a handwritten note of condolence to the family. They attend the funeral and pay their respects, even if the veteran has no family or friends in attendance.

There are one hundred and fifty of these special women. They are wives, widows and mothers of military personnel. The organization started in 1972, at the request of General Creighton Abrams. The general was passing a funeral that was in progress. He saw that no one was in attendance but the honor guard. General Abrams was upset. He vowed that from that day on, no veteran ever again would go to his grave alone in Arlington. That is why the Arlington Ladies were organized. The Arlington Ladies are special people and should be honored and cherished for what they do — they pay final homage to our fallen veterans.

These special ladies make it easy to see why so many law enforcement officers attend a fallen comrade's funeral. Law enforcement does not have Arlington Ladies'. Law enforcement officers have their families and each other. Members of the law enforcement community will not let a fellow officer go alone to his final resting place. Law enforcement officers take care of our own.

Perhaps if the American public took the time, they could learn how important honor and respect really are from their law enforcement officers. Maybe if the public had the same sense of courtesy and respect that law enforcement officers do, there no longer would be a need for the Arlington Ladies.

Many are curious about this small Las Vegas Nevada group which does so much for the community. Who are they and why do they do this?

First, the Wednesday Warrior Writers is a small group of friends who have a common interest, writing.

Next, Most all are former police officers, first responders and/or former military service members. Several are both.

This small group of friends wanted to assist young writers in their endeavors without them having to make the same mistakes they had in some cases. Looking for a venue to do these free presentations, we contacted the Clark county Library and was provided the space however, we had to have a group name, Being creative, and the fact that we met on Wednesdays, we created the name Wednesday Warriors, then added Writers because it is what we did.

THE CONTRIBUTING AUTHORS AND MEMBERS OF THE WEDNESDAY WARRIOR WRITERS OF LAS VEGAS NEVADA:

KEITH BETTINGER

Keith Bettinger is a retired Suffolk County, NY Police Officer. He's been writing for law enforcement publications for over 30 years and has received many awards for his articles, stories, poems and book. Keith has a monthly column in PoliceOne.com titled Musings of a Retired Cop. He has a Master's Degree in Human Relations with a major in Clinical Counseling. During his career he received the department's Bravery Medal, Silver Shield Award, Meritorious Police Service Award, Special Service Award, Professionalization Award, Department Recognition Award, 5 Headquarters commendations and six Precinct commendations. He also was a field training officer, Crime Prevention Officer and an instructor on Post Shooting Trauma and Critical Incidents. He was instrumental in the development of a Peer Counseling Program for Officers Involved in Critical Incidents. He also did debriefings of police officers who were at "Ground Zero" following the tragedies of September 11, 2001. Keith has written two books, **Fighting Crime with "Some" Day and Lenny**, **Murder in McHenry** and **End of Watch**. He has also contributed stories to the following anthologies; Cop Tales 2000, Charity, True Blue, To Protect and Serve, and Dad's Bow Tie. Keith has approximately 100 articles published in various publications in the United States and Canada. He also shares with Jack Miller, the screenplay **The Master Cheat**. He has received numerous writing awards for his short stories.

ROBERT M. CAWLEY

Robert Cawley is a diversified Production Executive, Creator, Writer, Producer, and Director whose TV programs won twenty Emmy Awards.

Hits include **Peter Marshall – One More Time," "My Little Corner of The World"** winner of the Freedoms Foundation and American Family Heritage awards, with Bob Hope, Anita Bryant

General William Westmoreland, Efrem Zimbalist, Jr. and the West Point Glee Club and Corps of Cadets, "**This Is Your FBI**," miniseries For NBC earned him a Department of Justice citation. He added an Angel Award for "**How to Change Your Life**" with Robert Stack and Rena Winters as hosts. His documentary "**AIDS: the Global Explosion**" was nominated for a Primetime Emmy.

Motion pictures include "**Treasure of Tayopa**," "**Glory Road**" and "**Butterfly,**"

Nominated for three Golden Globe Awards including "Best Picture."

A member of both the Greenbrier Military Junior College and Columbus Musicians Hall of Fame.

He is the author of four novels. "**Treasure of La Dura**," "**Terrorist Tayopa**," "**Southwest Adventure**" and the true crime classic "**Components of Murder**."

Contributing author to an anthology of patriots and heroes, "**I Pledge Allegiance**," sponsored by the Wednesday Warriors Writers group.

He has served as TV and Motion Picture Consultant to the College of the Arts at Ohio State University and the Republic of Bophuthatswana, South Africa.

He has taught at the University of Southern California, Columbia College of Los Angeles and currently teaches at the College of Southern Nevada.

He makes his home in Las Vegas.

RON CORBIN Phd

Ron Corbin was an Army helicopter and instructor pilot, serving two tours in Vietnam as a combat aviator. He received numerous unit and individual ribbons for combat action, to include being awarded the Air Medal 31 times; once with "V" device for valor. Honorably discharged in 1969, he joined LAPD as a policeman and pilot/instructor pilot for Air Support Division. Retiring after an on-duty helicopter accident, he finished his college and graduate education. He holds a Masters in Elementary Education and a PhD in Security Administration; with an emphasis in terrorism threats to America's nuclear resources.

He has over thirty years in law enforcement and private security with experience involving training, auditing and consulting at the local, state and federal levels of both government and private corporate entities. Ron was selected to be part of an armed executive protection detail for Arabic royalty during the 1984 Summer Olympics in Los Angeles. For several years, Ron was a member of a team of private security specialists who consulted to the Department of Energy. His responsibilities included conducting site vulnerability assessments, auditing and developing operational procedures, writing and performing crisis management exercises, participating as an adversary in force-on-force and limited scope exercises, and instructing tactical training and counter-terrorism skills for security forces at major DOE and plutonium enrichment facilities around the country. For some of this work, he was made an "honorary" captain for the New Orleans Police Department, and commissioned a Colonel and Aide-de-Camp on Louisiana Governor's Strategic Petroleum Reserve Security Task Force.

Joining the Las Vegas Metropolitan Police Department (Metro) in 1993 as a crime prevention specialist, Ron's specialty was Crime Prevention Through Environmental Design (CPTED), and he attended training in this discipline at The National Crime Prevention Institute at the University of Louisville. His CPTED subject matter expertise led to him being interviewed in "Reader's Digest," "Sunset Magazine," "Petromart Business," and Las Vegas Life" magazines. He also was responsible for publishing Metro's in-house training journal, the "Training Wheel." Ron has been a contributing columnist to "Las Vegas Now" magazine, as well as a guest lecturer on Royal Caribbean International cruise lines, addressing citizens' personal safety issues.

Ron is a multi-award winning writer for the PSWA (Public Safety Writers' Association). His break-out book, **Beyond Recognition**, is a memoir of his LAPD helicopter crash. He is a contributing author of stories published in **True Blue** (Sutton: vol. 1 & 2); **Felons, Flames and Ambulance Rides** (PSWA); **We Gotta Get Out of This Place** (Lazares: vol. 1-3).

Ron and his wife Kathy have three children and live in Las Vegas, NV. www.rcorbinsecurityauthor.com

ROBERT FREGEAU

Robert Fregeau is a twenty-three year veteran of the U.S. Air Force and a fifteen year retired member of the Nevada Department of Public Safety/Parole and Probation. Robert is a novice author working on his first full-length novel. His first published works appear in this anthology. During his military career he traveled worldwide as a crewmember assigned to B-52 and KC-135 aircraft while assigned to the Strategic Air Command (SAC). He is a Vietnam veteran.

As an adult parole and probation officer, Robert served in field supervision units with the Intensive Supervision Unit (ISU). He supervised the Las Vegas warrant unit and house arrest units during his tenure in the department. In addition, he was assigned duties as liaison with the Las Vegas Metropolitan Police Department. Robert joined the Fraternal Order of Police in 1990 and has served with distinction as state and local secretary, treasurer and trustee for more than fifteen years.

Robert's breakout novel is tentatively entitled *P.O.* It is about a retiring Navy SEAL who uses the knowledge gained in the military to enter a second career as a parole and probation officer in Las Vegas. The opening relates a formidable family crisis and culminates in a scenario whereby the hero must evaluate his own moral and ethical values. From the initial feedback the author has received, the novel will be a formidable read.

Robert currently resides in Las Vegas, Nevada with his family.

DENNIS GRIFFIN

Dennis Griffin retired in 1994, after a 20-year career in investigations and law enforcement in New York State. He and his wife Faith moved to Las Vegas, Nevada, shortly afterward. He wrote his first novel, **The Morgue**, in 1996. He currently has seven mystery/thrillers published.

Dennis's debut in non-fiction, **Policing Las Vegas – A History of Law Enforcement in Southern Nevada**, was released in April 2005. It covers the evolution of law enforcement in Las Vegas and Clark County from the City's establishment in 1905. His second non-fiction, **The Battle for Las Vegas – The Law vs the Mob**, tells the story of the Tony Spilotro era in Las Vegas from 1971 through1986. It was released in July 2006 and was a Computer Times Editor's Selection in October 2006. It was used as a textbook at Purdue University's organized crime course in the fall semester of 2010. **Battle** was followed by *CULLOTTA*, the biography of former Chicago and Las Vegas mobster Frank Cullotta. His latest effort is as co-author of **Surviving the Mob,** the biography of former Gambino crime family associate Andrew Didonato. The book was released in January 2011.

Dennis is currently a co-host of the Blog Talk Radio show **Crime Wire,** and a Managing Member of BEAR Media Consultants. He also serves as a consultant to the Vegas Mob Tour. He is an active member of the Public Safety Writers Association and Sisters in Crime.

SCOTT DECKER

Scott Decker retired from the FBI after a career investigating everything from stolen property to international terrorism. He began as a Special Agent on the Boston Office's Bank Robbery Task Force. From there he was promoted to the FBI's new Hazardous Materials Response Unit as its fourth member. On September 12, 2001, he led a team of FBI Hazmat Officers to Ground Zero where they established a command post at the edge of the fallen World Trade Center buildings.

He returned from New York to head up a squad of agents—each with an advanced degree in science—at the Washington Field Office where they coordinated the forensic components of the 2001 anthrax attack investigation. In 2009, he and his group were awarded the FBI Director's Award for Outstanding Scientific Advancement.

Decker retired from the FBI in 2011 and holds a doctorate in human genetics. His first book, *Recounting the Anthrax Attacks: Terror, the Amerithrax Task Force and the Evolution of Forensics in the FBI*, is due for publication in the fall of 2017.

CHARLES McKEE

Charlie was born in Raton, New Mexico and raised in Northern California. He holds an MPA degree; and is retired from a California college. His occupational service includes the Oakland Police Department, and as a sergeant with the Contra Costa County

Sheriff/Coroners department. He organized and managed a college security/campus police department, and also managed and taught at a Northern California police academy. Charlie served in the US Navy, US Army Reserve, and the California State Military Reserve (State defense forces). He is a graduate of the National Crime Prevention Institute (Louisville); Marksman Instructors Institute (LASU) and the Terrorism course at Camp San Luis Obispo. He co-authored Security Training: A Professional Approach; and is published in Police, Military and Survival magazines. He is a co-author in the anthology "I Pledge Allegiance", and is also published in "The 1958 Quemoy Crisis" An Oral History (Ministry of National Defense-MND-ROC). Charlie has been married for forty seven years; and has a daughter and four grandchildren.

JACK MILLER

Jack entered the US Army in 1955 and performed duties as a prison guard at US Disciplinary Barracks, Fort Gordon, Georgia. He was transferred and served as a town patrolman in Detroit Michigan. He enlisted in the US Air Force in 1958 where he performed security functions including nuclear weapon security within the Air Defense Command. In 1965 he accepted an assignment as a special agent of the Office of Special Investigations conducting criminal and counter-intelligence and counter-espionage investigations. He retired in 1975 as a Senior Master Sergeant. He accepted employment with the Clark County District Attorney's office as a special agent working undercover with local police and federal agencies conducting sting operations, and surveilling organized crime associates. He applied for and was accepted to be a special agent of the Nevada State Gaming Control Board and became an expert in cheating and cheating detection and testified at numerous State and Federal trials. In 1988 he retired from the NSGCB and created a gaming consulting company designing casino security systems and training security officers. In 2002 he fully retired and began writing and publishing novels based on based on actual events **Cold War Warrior** follows the recruitment of an airman by the Soviets to be a spy. **Cold War Defector,** a sequel to Warrior continues the story of the Soviet spy handler. **The Master Cheat** follows a group of casino cheats that net millions of dollars using various cheating techniques. **Operation Switch** and describes the first long term undercover police sting netting burglars, prostitutes, car thieves and murderers. **The Medal** concerns a reluctant soldier who has troubles while attempting to qualify for a Good Conduct Medal. **Sin City Indictment** describes the cases heard by a Clark County Grand Jury on which Jack served during 2012 and 2013.**The Peacekeepers** describes life on isolated radar stations of the USAF, the proceeds from the sale of this book are donated to the Air Force Radar Site Museum in Bellefontaine, Ohio. He has written several screenplays and anthologies. Jack has given free classes to persons who desire to be writers so they may avoid the pitfalls of the writing and publishing industry.(www.retafsa.com)

MERLE SAVAGE

Merle lived in Alaska when the Exxon Valdez oil spill occurred. She was hired along with many others to assist in the clean up. Merle was not a big lady, but rather petite, at five foot five and 130 pounds. Initially she worked the beaches picking up dead fowl and steam cleaning the rocky beaches. She was promoted to manage a boat which went close to shore to pick up the plastic bags loaded with the dead oily fowl. Many time she rejected bags from the big burly men because they were not secured properly and would leak onto her boat. While they were not happy with this little girl telling them what to do, they did it. Her next promotion came as manager of a tender where the beach crews slept, were fed and were supplied with the equipment necessary for them to do their job. Many of the workers praised Merle for the job she did in getting them the supplies such as masks to prevent them from breathing the fumes and odors of the crude oil.

To document much of this, she wrote a book titled **Silence in the Sound,** a revealing expose' of their futile attempts to clean up the spill.

In 2011 Merle passed away from a lung disease most probably brought on by the work she did during the clean up. She did fulfill another item on her bucket list, being alive long enough to celebrate her birthday of November 11. She wanted to see that date which she called her "picket fence" date, 11-11-11. We miss you Merle.

Wednesday Warrior Writers

MARSHAL "TONY" TAYLOR

Marshal Taylor lives in Las Vegas, Nevada with his wife of forty-nine years, Patsy Taylor. He has self-published three books: **Blossoms of Sin**, a coming of age story about a young man who feels he may have to shoot someone, **The Amargosa Blues**, a tale about the intersections of a teenager, a small desert town, and a Buntline Special pistol, and **A Fatal Misunderstanding**, which involves a retired would-be mystery writer with an old crime that casts a long shadow. His books are available on Kindle as well as through Amazon. Taylor is currently writing on a sequel to **The Amargosa Blues**, with the working title, **Maskerade**. The story revisits the small town deputy sheriff, Mel Embry and his desert community of Amargosa Springs.

Marshal Taylor was the co-publisher and editor of the **Spring Mountain Gazette**, a hometown newspaper for the small communities in the Spring Mountains around Las Vegas. He has published articles in the **Tournaments Illuminated** publication of the Society for Creative Anachronism, Inc., as well as contributing a series of articles in a local newsletter. He also has a blog, marshaltaylor.com, where he writes a travelogue titled **The Dinologs**, which he then publishes on line.

Marshal Taylor graduated from University of Nevada, Las Vegas. Along with dipping his toe into journalism, he has worked as an art director, commercial photographer, and as a Parks Planner for the City of North Las Vegas. When he is not writing, he volunteers for an adult literacy program, dabbles in gardening, and is a member of the Society for Creative Anachronism, where he studies period rapier fighting and occasionally does calligraphy.

RENA C. WINTERS

Multi-talented Rena Winters has enjoyed an outstanding career in the entertainment industry as a writer, talent, producer, production executive and as a major TV and Motion Picture executive.

Her writing ability won the coveted Angel Award for the "outstanding family TV special, "**How to Change Your Life**," which she co-hosted with Robert Stack. She wrote the two hour script (and co-produced) for "**My Little Corner of the World**," winner of the Freedoms Foundation and American Family Heritage awards.

Feature films include "**The Boys Next Door**," "**KGB, the Secret War**," "**Charlie Chan & the Curse of the Dragon Queen**" and "**Avenging Angel**."

Her producing credits include "**The Juliet Prowse Spectacular**" for 20th Century Fox, "**Sinatra - Las Vegas Style**" and "**Peter Marshall - One More Time**," which produced a best selling soundtrack album.

As Executive Vice President, she headed the entire USA operation for the international entertainment giant, Sepp-Inter, producers of TV Series, TV Specials, Feature Films and all areas of merchandising for their animated entities including "**The Smurfs**," "**Flipper**," "**Seabert**," "**The Snorks**" and "**Foofur**" (all Emmy Award winners) plus "**After School Specials**" for CBS-TV.

Author of the bestselling book "**Smurfs: The Inside Story of the Little Blue Characters**" currently available on Amazon and Kindle and in all book stores.

Her new book "**In Lieu of Therapy**," released October, 2014, an inspirational and uplifting read for busy people, currently available Amazon and Kindle and in all book stores.

Contributing author to an anthology of patriots and heroes, "**I Pledge Allegiance**," sponsored by the Wednesday Warriors Writers group currently on Amazon and Kindle.

She makes her home in Las Vegas, Nevada and works in her spare time as an editor and ghostwriter.